"In *The Roar Within*, Brent Henderson skillfully uses the best tool for helping men of all ages clearly understand biblical truths that transform. That tool is storytelling, and Brent is a master. Brent's unforgettable experiences, along with some well-chosen experiences of others, will guide you to not only why but how to apply the wisdom packed into the chapters. Read it and roar!"

**Steve Chapman**, author of *A Look at Life from a Deer Stand*

"*The Roar Within* is an adventure book with a purpose. It captured me with breath-holding stories ranging from Africa to Alaska and set me free with the paramount teaching of the Bible—that the power of God is at work within me. This excellent book awakens me to the fact that I am more than I realize. This is a book every man needs to read!"

**Dr. Jimmy Sites**, producer and host of
*Spiritual Outdoor Adventures TV*

"*The Roar Within* is a must-read for men. It is compelling, a page-turner, and brilliant in speaking directly to the things that take us out as men and help us live out of who God says we are. Brent is unique in his ability to weave together entertaining adventures as a professional outdoorsman with incredible wisdom as a seasoned leader, and his humility, honesty, and wisdom are both inspiring and refreshing."

**Robby Angle**, president and CEO of Trueface.org

"Our culture's onslaught against righteous masculinity is Satan's strategy to destroy men's role as image-bearers of God. But God has raised up His spokesmen. One such warrior for truth is Brent Henderson. *The Roar Within* exposes the emasculating lies of the enemy and boldly proclaims God's life-changing words that every man must hear: you are enough! A compelling, victorious adventure and a must-read for every Christian man!"

**Russell Thornberry**, *Buckmasters Magazine* editor-in-chief (retired), founder of Wildman, and international pastor at River's Edge Fellowship, Alberta, Canada

"I have known and partnered with Brent for a number of years, and what I and the men within my influence love about him is his ability to combine fascinating, true life experiences with genuine humility and terrific insight. True to form, *The Roar Within* is for every guy who has either lost or never found his true voice—the one God predestined for him to declare His authority over any opposition to His heart and legacy."

**Randy (RT) Phillips**, former president of Promise Keepers and men's pastor at Life Austin Church, Texas

"Through this book of great adventures, Brent invites you to join him in his greatest adventure—the discovery of trusting God with yourself."

**Bill Thrall**, cofounder of Trueface.org and coauthor of *The Cure*

"A must-read! *The Roar Within* is every man's survival guide to help navigate the wilds and chaos within him. This book brings to light what kills a man on the inside while providing hope and practical methods to defeat these 'man-killers.' It gives a voice and supernatural strength to the subdued spirit or 'roar' within a man's heart that, once found and released, provides the courage, strength, and passion to lead himself, his family, and others according to God's original design for a man. Be prepared for a wild, riveting ride . . . and find a comfortable spot, because right from the first paragraph, you will not be able to put this book down."

**Russell Peck**, Palm Coast, Florida, law enforcement officer (retired), outdoor enthusiast, and ministry leader

"In *The Roar Within*, Brent Henderson masterfully and insightfully dismantles the false narratives men have been taught and begins replacing lies with truth. I've had the honor to know, travel with, and share experiences with Brent in some pretty extreme environments. Through these experiences, both physical and spiritual, I've come to the place (as all men do eventually) of asking myself, 'Who am I really, where is my true value, and am I enough?' *The Roar Within* takes you on a journey of self-discovery in search of those answers."

**Ken Dodson**, president of True North Ventures, Inc.

"If I were you, I would read this book! Whether you are a non-believer, a new Christian, or have been a believer for decades,

*The Roar Within* will give you great insight into the love of God and the joy that comes from knowing who you are. No matter where you are in your life's journey, the wisdom of this book will expose the devil's lies and guide you to the joy God intended for you. Enjoy Brent Henderson's labor of love and rejoice in finding your *roar*!"

**Will Primos**, founder of Primos Hunting

"As a wife, a mom of two boys who are now grown men, a grandmother to two little boys, and a woman working in a mainly male industry, I'm still learning about how God uniquely wired men. After reading *The Roar Within*, I feel a great sense of relief realizing I don't have to dampen the spirit of adventure of the men in my life; it's inborn for a purpose. It's so crucial that our boys have an earthly father who has his focus on his heavenly Father. Each man has to find the confidence that only Christ can give and, in turn, find the roar within that God wants him to share with the world. I highly recommend this book to all women to help them understand the warrior, protector, and adventurer buried in the heart of every man, because it will free you to be the woman God made you to be."

**Lisa Bevill**, contemporary Christian musician

# THE
# ROAR
# WITHIN

# THE ROAR WITHIN

### UNLEASHING THE POWERFUL TRUTH OF WHO YOU REALLY ARE

## BRENT HENDERSON

Revell

a division of Baker Publishing Group
Grand Rapids, Michigan

© 2021 by Brent Henderson

Published by Revell
a division of Baker Publishing Group
PO Box 6287, Grand Rapids, MI 49516-6287
www.revellbooks.com

Printed in the United States of America

Library of Congress Cataloging-in-Publication Data
Names: Henderson, Brent, author.
Title: The roar within : unleashing the powerful truth of who you really are / Brent Henderson.
Description: Grand Rapids, Michigan : Revell, a division of Baker Publishing Group, [2021] | Includes bibliographical references.
Identifiers: LCCN 2020042206 | ISBN 9780800738938 (cloth)
Subjects: LCSH: Christian men—Religious life. | Christian men—Conduct of life.
Classification: LCC BV4528.2 .H46 2021 | DDC 248.8/42—dc23
LC record available at https://lccn.loc.gov/2020042206

21  22  23  24  25  26  27       7  6  5  4  3  2  1

# Contents

# Introduction

## THE ROAR WITHIN

Oh, the power revealed the first time the lion cub roared—
and understood who he really was.

One of the scariest nights I have ever spent was in a small fenced-in camp in Balule, South Africa, on the southern banks of the Olifants River in Kruger National Park. At night you can hear whole prides of lions roar—it's *awesome*.

As the African sun began to set, the flickering glow of the campfire illuminated a wide circle. The shadows of the night crept in and sparks drifted skyward. My tent was pitched just feet away from the edge of a barbed wire–topped chain-link fence, and I grilled hamburgers over the open flame. The intoxicating aroma of burning flesh cast a spell on man and beast for miles around as it swirled about and drifted into the night. When the final glimmer of daylight had melted away, the temperature dropped and blackness descended, as if I were sinking into the depths of the darkest sea.

While I was finishing the last few bites of meat, something caused me to pause and squint past the glow of the fire into the shadows. I sensed something was locked onto me before I had visual recognition; it's an intimidating feeling. Through the fog of the night and the drifting smoke—there, only twenty feet away, a ghostly pair of yellow eyes three feet off the ground was staring straight at me. I was totally paralyzed. Silent fear set in as the hairs stood up on the back of my neck; I could feel "fight-or-flight" begin to pump through my veins. Whatever had me in its sights was tracking my every move, and my eyes strained to uncover the predator blending into the night.

Moments seemed like minutes. Then all at once, the eerie shape of a large spotted hyena materialized; it had smelled the meat and was moving in on its prey. The jaws of a hyena can crush the pelvis of a buffalo in one bite. Knowing I was its intended victim was no small thing.

The hyena moved in my direction only to pause and urinate against the fence just feet from my tent to mark its territory. It became a game. I moved to where it had urinated and marked my territory. Within minutes it was back reclaiming its territory. This game of dominance, with the hyena moving in and out of the shadows, continued for about twenty minutes, when suddenly the hyena's body language changed from dominance to submission as it cowered and disappeared into the dark. I thought I'd won our game of "king of the hill" until my ears picked up on the true cause of its turning. In the distance, but moving closer, I heard the unmistakable sound of a lion pride roaring, claiming its territory. A male lion is extremely protective of his home and family; he uses his roar to warn off anything that might threaten them. Male lions have been known to take down an animal weighing several thousand pounds and can eat the equivalent of seventy hamburgers in a single sitting. Their ferocious roars can be heard five miles away, and when the whole pride sounds off, every living creature stops what it's doing. They all know who the real king of the African plains is. This king is not a thief; he rules the plains, protects his pride, and takes what is his.

## Finding Your One True Voice

A lion's roar isn't something it earns from its father or from how many kills it achieves. That roar is something a lion is born with. It's imputed. The roar is given to the lion by the One who created it.

This book is about helping you find your roar, your one true voice, the real *you* God placed in you the moment you truly believed—the you that is *Christ in you*. Not the flesh and bones walking around afraid, insecure, and full of worry and doubt, but the you from whom, when you live from that place, the enemy tucks tail and runs.

We are embarking on a journey—a safari to help men answer the Big Question: *Am I enough?* When you understand who you really are in Christ, you can live life to the full, the way that God intended.

> The thief comes only to steal and kill and destroy; I have come that they may have life, and have it to the full. (John 10:10)

Are you ready to unleash the powerful truth of who you really are? Are you ready to discover and release the roar within? Then it's time to dress for battle and get your game face on. Let's do this!

# 1

# The Big Question

The LORD is a warrior;
The LORD is His name.
EXODUS 15:3 NASB

The dark, rolling waves crashed against our boat, slamming us into the side of the large scow we were tied up to miles out in the open ocean of Bristol Bay, Alaska. Above the sounds of the smashing waves, I heard an argument breaking out on the deck of the scow. The voices were those of our captain and a deckhand from the larger scow, and things were getting out of hand quickly. As I was working to keep our boat steady, the captain's son was on a rope ladder above me, peering over the side of the scow to see what was causing this heated exchange. The next thing I knew, the son jumped off the rope ladder onto the deck of our boat, ran for the stern, opened a compartment below deck, and moments later burst out from behind the cabin door with a loaded AR15.

Several days before, there had been an altercation between our captain and this deckhand as we unloaded our catch onto this same scow. The deckhand's job was to weigh the $30'' \times 30'' \times 40''$ brailer bags full of salmon, each about a thousand pounds, to know how much to pay us once we totaled the weight of all the bags. The problem was the deckhand hadn't zeroed the scale and was trying to cheat us out of a lot of money—salmon isn't cheap.

When the salmon are running, sleeping even an hour or two is a luxury. Around-the-clock fishing for five days straight leaves everyone exhausted and on edge. Having to function at a high level with very little food or sleep, on dangerously cold, rolling seas, and smelling like a fishery gut pile makes for short, nasty tempers. When fishermen come ashore after being at sea for days or weeks, trouble is a sure thing. These small fishing villages attract a lot of people who just don't fit in the lower 48 (and a few who, like me, were just looking for an adventurous way to earn some money before the daily grind of college). For some of them, the wiring upstairs has a few faulty connections. Gambling, prostitution, heavy drinking, and illegal drugs were all there for the finding, and fights between these rough-cut hotheads were a given. When we had last been ashore, we'd gotten a burger at a hole-in-the-wall called the Red Dog Saloon, and we heard that the night before a couple of coked-up guys got into a knife fight, resulting in one man losing an ear. This was not a place you wanted to take your kids; you took a large handgun instead. It didn't take much to light someone's fuse, and they were all too ready to strike that match.

I guess I should clarify something. The devious deckhand wasn't a man; she was the roughest, smelliest woman I'd ever seen. I could only guess that when her ship made it to port, her shampoo of choice was Rogaine and her washrag was 40 grit sandpaper. She could outdrink a camel and was hairier than a muskox, meaner than a Cape buffalo, and more foulmouthed than a turkey vulture. The reason my buddy had gone for the AR15 was that he'd seen his dad shove this cheating deckhand hard onto the deck after she'd attempted to pull a knife on him.

Before the mayhem escalated into shots being fired, the captain of the scow burst onto the deck, grabbed the deckhand, and escorted her to her quarters. The captain instructed us to leave to help defuse the situation, and also let us know that she was being fired and would be on the next supply ship headed to shore.

On land or at sea, things in Alaska can go south quickly, and you'd better be able to handle yourself or you'll find yourself in a life-or-death situation on the count of one. Alaska isn't for sissies; only those who are wild at heart can survive there.

As crazy as that encounter was, I was strangely drawn to the new chapter of which I was now a part. It was almost as if I were taking the exam to get my man card, and I'd survived the first trial—at least as a character in a much larger story. I was being battle-tested, and something inside of me was beginning to step up. My boyhood question was being answered: Do I have what it takes to be a man?

> A man needs a much bigger orbit than a woman. He needs a mission, a life purpose, and he needs to know his name. Only then is he fit for a woman, for only then does he have something to invite her into.[1]

In John Eldredge's book *Wild at Heart*, he states that all men need three key elements in their lives: "a battle to fight, an adventure to live, and a beauty to rescue."[2] When I first read the book in 2001, that message grabbed hold of me like nothing I'd ever heard. It wasn't churchy, it wasn't girly; it awakened the masculine in me the way that building forts, playing army or cowboys and Indians, and exploring the mountainside behind my house as a young boy had done. Most men I talk to who have read *Wild at Heart* say they felt the same way I did: *finally*, a message for men that wasn't feminized, watered down, or politically correct—that gave men permission to be men.

While attending a Wild at Heart men's conference in Colorado in 2004, I had a conversation with John Eldredge about purpose. I felt embarrassed as I shared, "John, I'm here because I've lost my heart. I'm forty-four years old, and I'm not sure what I'm supposed to be doing with my life. I've always done what I thought everyone else thought I should be doing, but that pursuit has left me feeling like I'm just trying to please other people. I've lost the truest part of who I really am and what makes me come alive." I remember the next thing he said to me, because it moved me to my core in a way that nothing ever had before. He told me to stop asking myself what the world needed but instead ask myself what made me come alive, because what the world needs is men who have come alive.

When I was flying home from that conference, God spoke to me on the plane and told me that I would be his "warrior poet." What did that mean? What was I supposed to do? How long would it take? That title would change my life forever, but it would be almost ten more years before I would not only understand it but believe it.

Men ask the really deep questions when they are alone. *Why am I here? Who am I really? What is my purpose in this life? Will I make a difference?* My thoughts ran those circles as I sat alone for many hours on the deck of that Alaskan commercial fishing boat, keeping watch on the nets as massive schools of salmon made their way from the open ocean back to the streams where they were formed. They were headed there for one purpose: to give life to the next generation.

There's an old Russian proverb: "If you chase two rabbits, you will not catch either one." When I heard it, it was like a punch in the gut, because that was me for many years. I'd chased so many rabbits—all of them good things—but I was almost no further along in getting my questions answered than when I'd begun chasing them many years before. Why? Because I had never been able to identify that *one thing*. I'd been living my life for the opinions of others. Once again, John's words pursued me: "Ask yourself what makes you come alive."

John had challenged me to ask *and* answer the Big Question. *What makes me come alive?*

What was it that made me come alive like a lion on the prowl? I discovered it was fighting for the hearts of men, writing about the adventures God had planned for me to draw men to Himself! I knew, because it roared inside me so loudly that I couldn't *not* do it. I was made to be His warrior poet!

But almost as quickly as I heard the roar of God telling me who I truly was at my core and what I was meant to do, I learned the enemy wanted that roar—that purpose—silenced. He knew that if I ever truly lived out of that place where God made me fully alive, I would be dangerous. Just as God had a plan for me before I was born, the enemy had a plan to keep me from understanding my true identity.

◀◀◀◀▷▷▶▶

And dying in your beds many years from now, would you be willing to trade all the days from this day to that for one chance—just one chance—to come back here and tell our enemies that they may take our lives, but they'll never take our freedom!

William Wallace (*Braveheart*)[3]

In my home office hangs a replica of the sword William Wallace carried in the movie *Braveheart*. It's the sword Wallace had slung across his back as he rode his horse back and forth in front of an army of his countrymen and spoke to them when they were about to abandon their place on the front line out of fear. That speech is my favorite movie scene of all time. Whenever I watch it, something inside me wants to step up, to be a part of something larger than myself. Just holding that Scottish claymore in my hands gives me a feeling of power, strength, and purpose.

When I brought the sword home and drew the fifty-five-inch broad-blade, double-edged sword from its leather sheath for the first time, my eight-year-old son gasped and his eyes widened as he asked, "Dad, can I go out and hit some trees with that?" That eight-year-old boy sensed that he was made for something larger than himself; it was instinctive for him to see if he could wield that mighty blade.

Seeing my young son attempting to swing that sword that was as tall as he was stirred some very deep emotions in me. On one hand, I was proud. *That's my boy!* But the next emotion was one I didn't see coming: *fear.* It rose from the pit of my stomach into my throat. I wasn't worried that he was going to hurt himself or damage the trees; this was something much deeper. I agonized over the question, Do I have what it takes not only to teach my son how to wield this sword but to help him fight the many battles he has yet to face, and to help him discover and pursue his purpose as he grows into a man? It was a fight-or-flight moment.

Many men have fled in those moments, leaving their sons to try to figure out life for themselves. They were never trained how to raise their sons with a sense of purpose, or they'd been wounded too many times in battle, which left them feeling alone and abandoned. A boy who lacks the proper training, challenges, and encouragement as he grows into manhood will rarely find his purpose in life. He will end up settling for a mundane, mediocre life, losing his heart one day at a time. Or he will find himself getting into trouble, constantly trying to prove he's a man by affairs, drinking, or the pursuit of money and fame. Never being taught how to wield the sword brings about a slow, purposeless death—dragging on one day at a time until he is nothing but a dead man walking.

Do you want to know God? Do you want to come alive? Do you want to know your purpose? Do you want to know your true name? Then you have to discover *the roar within*!

> They will walk after the LORD,
> He will roar like a lion;
> Indeed He will roar
> And His sons will come trembling from the west.
>   (Hos. 11:10 NASB)

## THE **BIG** QUESTION:

What is that one thing that you just can't *not* do—the one thing that makes you feel truly alive?

# 2

# Introducing the Big Five Man-Killers

On the wild plains of Africa, you're on the menu. It's a savage land that will quickly propel all your senses to high alert, and off-the-hook adventures are sure to fill the bill. One excellent location for these exploits is Kruger National Park in South Africa. If you put in the time, you stand a good chance of seeing Africa's Big Five—and if you get *too* close, you could even become part of the great circle of life. The Big Five are the rhinoceros, lion, Cape buffalo, elephant, and leopard. These man-killers are called the Big Five because of the difficulty in hunting them; they are five of the deadliest animals to walk the planet.

Being a big-game hunter, I have found myself in some pretty hairy situations on numerous occasions. When in the wilds, you have to remember that you are in their territory. You are constantly measuring each step, listening, smelling, feeling the wind's direction on your face, and watching for any movement.

It's imperative to pay close attention at all times, as a lapse in any of those areas can alert game to your presence, causing them to either flee from you or try to eat you for lunch. This is where you have to bring your A game.

And whether you realize it or not, everyday life is the same.

I recently asked a trusted group of over three hundred men to rate the top five struggles they deal with. I did this through a private "for men only" Facebook group I started called Dangerous Men. One of the rules is that what is shared in the group stays in the group. If a member breaks the rule, he is removed from the group; confidentiality is absolutely essential. Some of the men responded within my post, while others communicated with me privately, wanting to share their stories and explain *why* they put their struggles in a particular order. There are obviously more than five struggles men have, but of the ones I asked them about, here is how they rated them. I think you'll find it eye-opening.

1. Lack of purpose
2. Lack of respect
3. Anger
4. Lust
5. Shame

Next, I created an example of how each struggle can avalanche into the next. This may not be the same for you individually, but in staying true to the research, here is an illustration I believe most men will understand: when a man (1) lacks purpose, he doesn't feel good about himself, so he craves respect from his wife, friends, boss, and/or coworkers. If he perceives a (2) lack of respect, he becomes (3) angry. The anger can cause him to (4) lust, have affairs, look at porn, cuss, throw or hit things, or even quit his job. Those actions lead to (5) shame, which leads to more hiding or attempts at behavior modification. Realizing he can't conquer this on his own (can't "manage" his sin), he feels more shame, which eventually leads to more sin. Wash, rinse, repeat.

We struggle when we start comparing ourselves to others. This can create deep isolation, as it leads to low self-worth. The only answer to these struggles is when a man realizes that his worth and value will never come through what he did or didn't accomplish, whether he has others' respect, or whether he did or didn't sin. A man's identity in Christ will never come through his performance but only through *Christ in him*, which is something he cannot earn; it is a gift. God put His righteousness, His "good enough," in the believer the moment he truly believed. And *that*, my friend, is enough to take down any man-killer.

We're going to assign one of the Big Five deadly man-killers of the African plains to each of the big five man-killers men struggle with on the home front. These are the deadliest lies that stalk a man and want to destroy his heart. As we continue on our journey, we'll identify these man-killers and learn how to stop them in their tracks.

# The Big Five Man-Killers #1

## LACK OF PURPOSE

### *(Rhinoceros)*

Rhinos live a very isolated life. They are not social; they're solitary creatures. Their visual field reaches only about twenty-five feet, so they're not distracted by things they see. They go to the bathroom in the same spot, creating a dung pile the size of a Volkswagen, and they alternate between feeding and resting through the day and night. During the rare times when they aren't eating or sleeping, you'll find them getting a cool mud soak (their spa treatment). Rhinos have no desire to do anything but eat—unless something threatens their safety.

Several years ago, an African veterinarian was sedating rhinos so they could be examined and given vaccinations if needed. After a tranquilizer dart hit a four-thousand-pound rhino, the rhino quickly became irritated. The vet ran, thinking he'd been identified by the rhino as the source of that shot in the butt.

*Big* mistake—the rhino came at him like a bulldozer. As the vet tried to escape, the rhino dropped its head between the man's legs, and before he could jump out of the way, the rhino raised its head with so much force that the horn went clear through the vet's thigh as he was lifted off the ground. Then, lifting the 225-pound man off the ground again, the rhino tossed him back onto its second horn like a sack of potatoes, snapping his spine. As if that wasn't enough torture, the rhino then tossed the vet into the air like a rag doll while going through a thicket of acacia thorn trees. The thorns of the acacia are as long as your finger and as sharp as a hypodermic needle. Before his body could hit the ground, the vet was skewered by thorns and was suspended face-up until his partner could cut him out. After using the tools in their medical kit to close the gaping hole in his thigh, his partner called in a chopper to get him to safety.

In a heartbeat, that lethargic, bored beast had become a man-killer.

Lack of purpose, like the rhino, is a two-horned killer. It can manifest itself through lethargy or through acting out. In some, lack of purpose can look like laziness, causing a man to lose focus, shut down, or unplug from life and relationships. He may start sleeping excessively or suffer with feelings of depression. Lack of purpose can also cause a man to get caught up in something that makes him feel alive but is not good for him: overworking, overeating, excessive gaming, taking risks to get that adrenaline rush, giving in to sexual temptation, and so on. Lack of purpose always plays on a man's thoughts, making him believe he's not good enough. That belief can drive a man to sin. Sin always has an immediate payoff when we're feeling down—that's why it's so attractive. The problem is that it leaves us feeling even more worthless.

When a man lacks purpose and direction, he will not feel valued; this plays havoc with his psyche, causing him to wonder why he's here. In the movie *First Blood*, a decorated Vietnam war hero, John Rambo, struggles to find his purpose after the war. He becomes an antisocial drifter, unable to cope with the loss of the life, friends, and purpose he once knew. In one of the opening scenes, he's mistreated and talked down to by the local sheriff, who tells him that this community doesn't want drifters like Rambo in their town. He insults Rambo by mocking the way he looks while having the American flag on his jacket—the flag of the country Rambo had been willing to give his life to defend. He then tells Rambo that he wouldn't like it there because the town is boring, and proceeds to escort him to the outskirts of town to keep Rambo from being a part of that safe little community. It was the peace and freedom of these little towns that Rambo had fought to protect. During the war he had discovered a purpose larger than his own life to give himself to; now the very ones he fought for were labeling him a drifter and telling him he wasn't good enough.

One of the most gut-wrenching and powerful scenes is the end of the movie. Rambo is surrounded by hundreds of law enforcement officers attempting to either kill him or take him into custody when his commanding officer from the war shows up and attempts to de-escalate the conflict. He reminds Rambo that he had once been a part of an elite group and begs him not to let it end this way. Being reminded that he'd once been part of something special triggers a volatile response Rambo has been holding inside for years. "Back there I could drive a gunship! I could drive a tank! I was in charge of million-dollar equipment! Back here I can't even hold a job parking cars!"[1] The next thing you see is Rambo collapsing onto the floor, sobbing as he remembers. This once-elite warrior was now lying on the ground, lost. Purposeless.

Let's look again at William Wallace's speech.

> And dying in your beds many years from now, would you be willing to trade all the days from this day to that for one chance—just one chance—to come back here and tell our enemies that they may take our lives, but they'll never take our freedom![2]

What was it about this speech that moved men who were about to cut and run to pick up their weapons and charge the enemy? *Purpose.* When Wallace rode in on his horse, face painted for war, claymore at the ready, his voice full of passion and his words like a double-edged sword slicing apart the lies the men had unknowingly believed, something extremely powerful happened. There was a mighty turning of the tide. These men let out a mighty roar from a place deep within, a roar that had been waiting for such a time as this to be called up. They were ready to answer the question, Do I have what it takes? Their purpose had been awakened, and these men were ready to give their lives for something greater than themselves.

In the introduction, I shared how when the lion roared that night in Balule, the hyena cowered and ran because it knew what that lion was capable of doing. Why then do so many men run from their calling or duty and head into the shadowy places when *the Lion of Judah* is on their side? *Purposelessness.* When a man loses his sense of purpose, he feels like he is not enough, like he's in an endless bank of fog, alone, helpless and hopeless, and he'll run from the very battles and challenges he was designed to overcome. Lack of purpose is the number one man-killer all men face.

A man's purpose isn't manmade—it comes from God. What man didn't give, man can't take away. The only One whose opinion matters is God. Period. Because of God's gift of grace, a man doesn't have to dutifully or anxiously perform to please God. Creating our own purpose in an attempt to please God or others takes us away from what God wants and puts us in the place of being our own master.

Surrendering our lives to God allows us to joyfully and peacefully participate in the purpose He's planned for each of us. This purpose is not found through performance, achievement, recognition, or respect. Our true purpose can only be found through total surrender to *God's* purpose for us. That begins to happen when we start believing God is who He says He is and we are who God says we are.

When you take away a man's purpose, you've taken away his passion, his will to live, his identity. The problem occurs when we believe our purpose comes from what we do or what others think of us. That belief leads a man to take his *Do I have what it takes?* question to the wrong place. Where does he go with this question? To his performance and other people's opinions. When he fears not being enough, he will create an elaborate mask, displaying a false self to attempt to prove he's good enough.

## THE **BIG** QUESTION:

Where in your life do you find you're most tempted to put on the mask, and why?

# 4 Finding Your Swing

Inside each and every one of us is our one, true, authentic swing. Something we was born with. Something that's ours and ours alone. Something that can't be learned . . . something that's got to be remembered.

*THE LEGEND OF BAGGER VANCE*

*T*he *Legend of Bagger Vance* is the story of a golfer from Savannah, Georgia. Young golf hero Rannulph Junuh (played by Matt Damon) is a prodigy who by the age of sixteen is well on his way to becoming one of the most famous names in golf. Then WWI breaks out. Junuh enlists in the army and is soon shipped off to Europe, leaving his giftedness behind to fight in a horrible war. He comes out with a Medal of Honor, but since everyone else in his regiment is killed, he also comes out with a minefield of unhealthy thoughts from the horrors he experienced. Upon returning home, he discovers he's not only lost his friends and his girl, he's also lost his desire to ever again play the game he loved. Instead of picking up where he left off before the war, Junuh retires to an old farmhouse, where he sinks into a mire of heavy drinking, smoking, and gambling with guys who've lost their hearts as well, and essentially gives up on life.

During one such evening of drinking and gambling, a young boy named Hardy Greaves walks through the door in search of this golfer his father had once told him about—the best golfer he'd ever seen. The local golf course is putting on a tournament with a winning prize of $10,000. They've invited the two best golfers of the day, Bobby Jones and Walter Hagen, but a third player is required to complete the roster, and it must be a native of Savannah. The young boy thinks that bringing in Junuh would be their best hope of putting Savannah on the map. No one knows where Junuh is, but the persistent Hardy finds him—a little drunk, in a smoke-filled room, just a shell of a man. When Junuh asks Hardy what brings him here, the boy says maybe he should come back when Junuh's not so "busy." Junuh replies, "I thought you were going to say 'drunk,'" and informs the boy that there's not enough alcohol in the entire state to get him drunk enough. When Hardy asks him how drunk is drunk enough, Junuh replies that it's all a matter of brain cells.

Every drink of liquor you take kills a thousand brain cells. . . . First the sadness cells die, so you smile real big . . . then the quiet cells go, so you just say everything real loud for no reason at all. That's ok . . . because the stupid cells go next, so everything you say is real smart. And finally come the memory cells. These are tough . . . to kill.[1]

Just about anything—alcohol, food, drugs, sex, work, exercise, or even attending church—can become the means to kill our memory cells. If we can't atone for our sins by being religious enough (performance), we'll cultivate an addiction to bury them deep within.

## The Big Lie

One thing I know from working with people with alcohol problems is that they usually aren't drinking to get drunk for no reason. If you listen closely to what they're saying the more they drink, there is deep-seated pain buried far below the plastic exterior they are trying so hard to maintain. This pain has silenced more than a few good men. You might think the pain that begins to come out is from the loss of a job or a loved one or from a broken relationship. And if you look no deeper into what they're saying, then you'll think that's as deep as it goes—and that's exactly what the enemy wants. He doesn't want you digging any deeper, because if you do, you will see past his deception of "blaming self or blaming others" and get down to what's really happening. Satan is the one who is to blame.

Let me untangle that a bit. The Bible teaches in 1 Thessalonians 5:23 that we are made up of three parts: body, soul, and spirit. Our body is our flesh—it's what we can see. Our soul, contrary to popular belief, is not the eternal part of us but rather where our thoughts, will, and emotions are formed. Our spirit is the eternal part of us. That's the part of us the enemy can't touch once we're believers. The moment you truly believe and receive Christ as Lord and Savior, God's promised Holy Spirit comes into your spirit and dwells within you. That means that, at your core, you are *100 percent complete in Him*. God is the One who completes you and gives you your true worth and value, but the enemy doesn't want you to know that. If you could actually grasp this powerful truth—if this truth were to penetrate to the core of your being—it would radically change your life. Satan knows that, and will do all he can to stop that from happening.

So, how does the enemy keep us there? Here's his biggest lie:

**Your Performance + Others' Opinions = Your Self-Worth**

Satan traps you into believing that your "good enough" comes from your performance. He can do this by making you believe that if something difficult happens—for example, the loss of a job or relationship—you're a worthless loser. But he can take the opposite tack as well, convincing you that if something good happens—say, you get a promotion at work—this makes you great (and better than others, who are now worthless losers). This is how the enemy eats you for lunch, swallowing you whole over and over and over again.

If Satan can deceive you into believing your worth comes from others' opinions, with thoughts like, *If I were more of a man, she'd have sex with me more often*, or, *If I were more of a man, she wouldn't have left me*, he has you in the bag. Another lie is, *If I were bigger (or tougher, or more important), men would respect me more*. Or the lie may come through loss: *I'm divorced; no one will ever love me again.* That's another one of his cognitive distortions, called an all-or-nothing statement. If you buy into these lies, he'll chew you up and spit you out covered in the slime of depression and shame, leaving you seeking ways to deaden the pain through addictions or religion. Junuh's drug of choice was alcohol, which was probably the more honest of the two.

44<<>>>>

At first, Junuh does everything he can to dissuade Hardy's attempts to "convert" him, but the boy is relentless. Junuh turns young Hardy away, but something in the boy's belief in him reawakens a place deep in his soul, a place he thought was lost—forgotten—a place he'd buried when his get-up-and-go got up and went after the war. But now a new war is raging. Junuh's battle is now an internal one to once again believe in who he really is.

The dark of night finds Junuh outside of his house, alone with just a lantern and his golf clubs. As Junuh is hitting balls everywhere but straight, a stranger (played by Will Smith) mysteriously appears directly in front of him, like a ghost in the darkness. Junuh tells the man he could have killed him, and the man answers that with the shots Junuh was making, right in front of him was the safest place.

At first Junuh is taken aback by the boldness and truthfulness of this man, Bagger, whom he's never seen before. The two men begin to talk, and Bagger offers to be Junuh's caddy for the upcoming Savannah tournament, with Bagger's cut being only the guarantee of $5.00. Bagger sees something deeper than slices, hooks, and missed opportunities, and it's unsettling to Junuh. Suspicious, he thinks, *Yeah, right—what's the catch?*

Embarrassed and angry that this stranger has been watching him hit one bad shot after another, he hands Bagger a club and tells him to hit a ball. Bagger crushes a shot into the darkness, leaving Junuh dumbfounded and sullen. Junuh is not just frustrated by the fact that this guy is striking the ball better and farther than he is. He's puzzled that this total stranger wants to come alongside him to help him get his swing back—and for a guarantee of just five bucks.

When Bagger tells Junuh that the trick is to find his swing, a dumbfounded Junuh asks, "What'd you say?" As Bagger smiles and kneels to tee up another golf ball, he looks up at Junuh and simply tells him that he's lost his swing, and that they need to go find it.[2]

When Junuh uttered the words, "What'd you say?" the look on his face was as if someone had just turned the key to the core of his being, like he'd been seen for the very first time without flaw, without sin, without shame. Forgiven.

Years ago someone told me that if we invest in others, if we "add value" to them, we build trust. We draw others to us. That's exactly what Bagger was doing. Bagger came just for Junuh, as if it were a divine appointment from a higher power. It's like the way the Holy Spirit comes alongside each believer.

Sometimes all it takes for a man to find his swing—to find his roar again—is for someone to come alongside him and remind him who he really is and what he's capable of when he ditches the lies and replaces them with truth. Unfortunately, many men take their "swing" to a woman to get their affirmation, or hide in shame feeling like they're not good enough for her. Men also do this when they compare themselves to other men, leaving them feeling either more prideful or more pitiful than they should. Comparison is a losing game.

After the war, Junuh had retreated to his home and put himself in solitary confinement. He hid not only from the game he'd loved but from Adele, the woman he loved. The tournament, in which Junuh eventually agreed to play, had been Adele's idea; she was hosting the event hoping to revive both Savannah, Georgia, and her late father's golf resort.

The tournament begins. After the first round, Junuh's fallen far behind the leaders. It's so embarrassing, he's ready to quit and walk away. He's allowing everything around him to keep him from playing his game. Junuh watches his competitors connect with their shots, leaving the crowd in awe, and he's losing strokes on every hole as he begins to compare himself with them. Bobby Jones, the good-looking golfer with the perfect hair and swing, has won national championships, British Opens, and a Grand Slam. And while doing that, he earned an engineering degree from Georgia Tech, an English literature degree from Harvard, and a law degree from Emory. Walter Hagan has won national championships, British Opens, and PGAs; in one stretch he won twenty-two straight professional championships.

After Junuh's first-round meltdown, Adele apologizes to him. When he asks her what she's apologizing for, she answers it's for publicly humiliating him. Well, that's just *sure* to help his game—he's already comparing himself to the other players, and now the woman he loves emasculates him by pointing out how horribly he's playing! To a man who's struggling with his identity, that dumps some serious salt in the wound. In Junuh's heart of hearts, he desperately wants Adele. He's exhausted from dancing around the minefields of horrific memories, but he just can't shut it off. He needs someone who can reach deep within him, someone who can listen well and doesn't need anything from him. He thinks winning the girl is the answer to his question, but taking his question to her will never be enough.

Adele walks away, and young Hardy comes out from behind a tree where he's been hiding and listening. As they make their way to the clubhouse, Hardy tries to convince Junuh that if he can just pick up one stroke every four holes, he can get back in the game. He encourages Junuh not to let his current score keep him from giving his best. Then Hardy shares how humiliated he feels because his father lost his hardware store in the Depression and had to take the lowly job of street sweeper. Junuh tells him that his father is a good man and did the right thing—he didn't give up and declare bankruptcy like so many others, but he "stared adversity in the eye . . . and beat it back with a broom."[3] When Junuh says those words to Hardy, something clicks inside him. It's a wake-up call to stop wallowing in self-pity—to not let adversity beat him either. Junuh recognizes the lie he's been buying into that's keeping him from playing his game.

Bagger also realizes that it is Junuh's beliefs about himself that are robbing him of the focus and confidence he needs. All Junuh can think about is how many strokes he's behind, making him charge the hole as if he's slaying a dragon instead of concentrating on the shot in front of him. Junuh needs to be able to be still. In the moment. Focused. Bagger pulls him aside and tells him to watch how Bobby Jones prepares his mind for the next shot. Bobby's not thinking about past shots or future shots; he's thinking solely about the shot directly in front of him. He's focused. There are a lot of shots he could choose, but there's only one authentic shot, and it's going to choose Bobby. Bagger encourages Junuh that there's an authentic shot in every one of us—we just have to get out of the way and let it happen.

As play resumes, Junuh is eight strokes behind. Then something amazing happens—he starts playing his game. He gets an eagle and then a hole in one. Bagger has helped Junuh knock out the peripherals that had been clogging his thinking and keep his eyes only on the flag at the end of the fairway. Junuh has now found his swing, dazzling the crowd as he connects with each shot. But he struggles to connect emotionally with Adele. As Junuh walks down the course, Adele suddenly grabs him and pulls him behind a tree. Junuh has finally begun to experience feelings again and has started moving toward Adele. But not understanding what the war had done to him, Adele feels torn and a little used. Feeling forgotten by the man she loved, she declares that she can't understand why Junuh stopped corresponding with her for ten years. She can't understand what happened to him—to them. Obviously hurt, she tells him he'd never even said he was sorry—but when Junuh apologizes, Adele tells him it's too late for that.

Not getting what he needs from Adele, he shifts his *Do I have what it takes?* question away from her to the opinions of others. He's now playing for the cheers of the crowd. As the movie crescendos, Junuh is once again being applauded for his giftedness. He's only a few strokes behind the leaders. Floods of praise rise from the crowd as they can't believe what they're seeing; it's a Cinderella story.

What Junuh can't see is that the floods of praise for his talent are building into a tsunami of pride that could rob him of his swing and drown him in arrogance. Now desperate to impress the onlookers, especially Adele, Junuh's thoughts lead to more poor shots, and he once again falls behind Jones and Hagen. This time his bad shots are a result of striving to "wow" the crowd, trying to make himself look better so he'll feel better.

He's traded the pain-killing effects of alcohol for something more culturally respectable: the good opinions of others.

He's falling irreversibly behind. Junuh's next shot leaves him hitting from inside the edge of the woods, where he disappears from the crowd's view—almost as if that's his plan. He's ashamed and afraid that maybe he isn't who he thought he was. And the truth is, he's right. He has believed that who he is—his identity—is determined by his performance and by what people think of him. Junuh desperately needs a savior; his fallenness reveals to him that he can't save himself—that on his own, he's *not* good enough. As he looks at his situation, it feels hopeless. Memories of the war begin to crash in on him, creating fear and doubt, and he begins forgetting who he really is. Shaking from flashbacks, Junuh finds himself in the midst of a mental breakdown and about to quit.

In steps Bagger.

> JUNUH: I can't do this . . .
>
> BAGGER: What I'm talking about is a game—a game that can't be won, only played.
>
> JUNUH: You don't understand.
>
> BAGGER: I don't need to understand. Ain't a soul on this entire earth ain't got a burden to carry he don't understand—you ain't alone in that. But you been carrying this one long enough. Time to go on—lay it down.
>
> JUNUH: I don't know how.

BAGGER: You got a choice. You could stop, or you could start.

JUNUH: Start?

BAGGER: Walking.

JUNUH: Where?

BAGGER: Right back to where you always been—and then stand there—still—real still—and remember.

JUNUH: It's too long ago.

BAGGER: Oh no, sir—it was just a moment ago. Time for you to come on out of the shadows, Junuh. Time for you to choose.

JUNUH: I can't.

BAGGER: Yes, you can. But you ain't alone. I'm right here with ya. I been here all along. Now, play the game—your game—the one only you was meant to play—the one that was given to you when you come into this world. You ready? C'mon—take your stance. Strike that ball, Junuh—don't hold *nothing* back—give it *everything*. Now's the time. Let yourself remember—remember *your* swing—that's right Junuh—settle yourself—let's go. Now is the time, Junuh.[4]

As Junuh listens, remembers, and believes who he really is, he's able to focus and remember his swing. Bagger's words of encouragement and identity create the revelation Junuh needs to believe what is true about himself. Bagger was his "Holy Spirit." Junuh finds his swing—the one given to him by his Creator when he came into this world—and with confidence, he strikes that ball through a small gap in the trees, landing his shot just a few feet from the hole.

The moment Junuh believed, he unleashed his true potential. He quit hiding, stepped out of the shadows, took the leap, stopped taking his question to the wrong place, got back in the game, and played the best round of his life. That day, Junuh found his courage and stiffened his spine—and Savannah heard Junuh's roar within.

## THE **BIG** QUESTION:

Painful happenings in our past can rob us of our present. What difficult circumstances from your past has the enemy used to cause you to put on a mask? What does your mask look like?

# 5

# When Brave Men Stand

Courage is contagious. When a brave man takes a stand,
the spines of others are often stiffened.

BILLY GRAHAM

The winter winds were howling. It was a frigid northwest
Pennsylvania morning, and I had recently been hired to
be the worship leader of a church not far from where
I'd grown up. I was drawn back to my childhood stomping
grounds after being away for twenty years, not just by the call
of ministry but also the call of the wilds. I knew almost every
fishing honey hole, mountain ridge, and forest trail for miles.
My roots of adventure were planted deep in this area, and the
opportunity to come back and be a part of a large, growing
church was appealing.

When I arrived at the church in late summer, I was given additional responsibilities over and above my job description. Not only was I to develop and lead the worship teams but also I was asked to rebuild their choir, which had dwindled down to twelve people (mostly women), and to be over the WING (welcoming in new guests) ministry as well. I was also to supervise the ushers, greeters, sound techs, and creative arts: puppets, special music, and dance. I really have to laugh at that last one. I was a hunter and fisherman with two left feet—I only danced when I harvested a good buck or landed a monster trout or largemouth bass.

Being a glutton for punishment, I went to the staff after just six weeks and requested to start a men's ministry. Why would I do that? Because leading men was where I found my purpose—it's what made me come alive. On the Sunday they announced I'd be starting a men's program and that I was an avid hunter, men flocked to the back of the sanctuary after the service, wanting to know if I'd start an archery ministry. Within two weeks we had more than enough 3D targets donated to create an entire archery course. I'd tapped into something that was moving the men of this area, and they were all in.

One of the most stirring quotes I've read is from Billy Graham: "Courage is contagious. When a brave man takes a stand, the spines of others are often stiffened."[1]

Little did I know that just a month after getting this archery ministry started, an event I could not have foreseen began to draw out of me and the other men something we didn't know we possessed: courage.

## Running to the Battle

Nelson Mandela had an excellent explanation of courage. He said, "I learned that courage was not the absence of fear, but the triumph over it. The brave man is not he who does not feel afraid, but he who conquers that fear."[2]

Fear can leave you feeling cold. On one freezing January morning, a local college choir had been invited to do the music for our morning services, and their eager, smiling faces were incredibly refreshing to watch. It was a much-needed break for me to worship from the front pew, seated with the congregation.

The first service went off without a hitch. The choir performed several numbers, their eyes fixed on their conductor; they touched us with their smiles and moving melodies. But at some point during their performance in the second service, something changed. In the middle of one of their songs, to my left a man made his way down the side aisle and up the stairs and quietly moved dead center behind the choir. No one seemed alarmed yet, but something didn't feel right. He wasn't wearing a suit and tie, or even jeans and a flannel—the choice of many men from this area. He was dressed in camo pants, black military boots, a black leather jacket, and black gloves, and was brandishing a compound bow with a full quiver.

Suddenly, he raised the bow above his head and shouted, "I am an angel of the Lord! Anyone who doesn't repent, death will come to you!" I immediately glanced around the room, but to my surprise, no one was moving. Maybe they thought it must be a part of the performance, but this hadn't happened during the first service. Something was definitely wrong.

My eyes scanned the choir; their eyes were still fixed on their director and they continued to sing. As I looked at the top row of singers, a girl standing directly in front of the shouting man looked directly back at me. Sensing her fear, I mouthed, "Is he with you?" Trying not to cause a commotion, or perhaps paralyzed by fear, she mustered a slow side-to-side head shake to let me know something was terribly wrong. And something inside of me moved me to do what fear was telling me not to. Without hesitation, I crouched down, crept around the front of the choir, and made a dash for him. Later, my thoughts would be a barrage of what-ifs: *What if he'd had a handgun? What if he'd had a MAC-10 or an Uzi?* He could have taken me out, along with the choir and many in the congregation.

When he saw me coming across the back of the stage directly for him, instead of using his weapon, he ran down the side aisle toward the lobby. As I chased after him, I caught the eye of a police officer in our church seated to my left. That was all he needed to spring into action, as his heightened senses were already on alert. This 6'4" muscular beast of a man launched from his pew and was in the lobby on the count of one. When he met me there, I already had hold of the man, who was fighting against me and screaming that death would come to me, as he was an angel of the Lord. I'll never forget the words that came out of my mouth: "Buddy, you ain't no angel!"

As I held on to the man, the officer was already on the phone calling it in. When I released my grip, one of the ushers grabbed the guy and shoved him toward the front doors. That's all he needed to escape. Instead of running to the nearest door, he tore down the side hall and out another door with me in pursuit, then headed back toward the front of the church. I couldn't figure out why he ran that way until I rounded the corner of the building. Parked against the front doors of the church was his pickup truck; he had pulled it up so it pressed against the main entry doors, which would have kept people from being able to escape in a panic.

By the time I caught up to him, he was in his truck and starting the engine. As I jumped around the tailgate of his truck to get his plate number, he threw it in reverse and tried to run me over. His spinning tires squealed, and the smell of burned rubber filled the entryway as he took off. Knowing I couldn't run him down on foot, I ran back into the church and informed the officer what had just happened. He got back on the phone, and an APB was put out on the white pickup.

At this point, I thought it was all over. I went back inside the church . . . and the college choir was still performing! Being a performer myself, I have to laugh at how focused you can be while you're onstage; "the show must go on."

After the service, I went to the state police and filed a report detailing what had taken place. Two days later, I was returning from lunch with the staff when the church secretary came running up all flustered. "He was here! The guy with the bow was just here!" As she was shouting, I spun around to make sure he wasn't somewhere behind me and saw his pickup parked in the middle of the lot. I shouted, "Where is he?" She answered that she'd called the police as soon as he had come into the building. They were nearby and on the scene in about a minute and had taken him into custody. The guy who on Sunday had been dressed in camo and black and carrying a bow was now dressed in an all-white robe and claiming to be a prophet, saying he'd been mistaken in thinking he was an angel. My next question was, "What did he say when he came in?" She told me he'd said he'd come to take me out to where he lived beside a lake, to prove to me that he could walk on the water. My response to her is one I still laugh at now, years later: "*I* can walk on the water—it's *January*!"

When I got back to my office, I called the police station to find out what was happening with the situation. They assured me he would be kept at least seventy-two hours for a psychological evaluation. Sometime during this period, two officers went to the location of the dwelling he'd wanted to take me to. When they peered through the window, they saw a shotgun wired to the front door that would have discharged upon opening. I knew that gun was intended for me. Immediately my thoughts began racing. Would he come after me if he got out after the psych eval? Would he come after my family? Fortunately, he was not released; instead, he would be held until his court case, where I would be the primary witness and would have to testify.

The day of the court appearance came, and my friend Greg accompanied me to the courtroom. When this guy saw me come in, he turned toward me and gave me a look with eyes that were empty and dark, like something out of a horror movie.

He was sentenced to one year in jail and ordered to write a letter to the church to apologize for his actions. He served his time, but no apology or letter was ever delivered. I recently heard through people who knew his family that he passed away a few years ago. Mental illness is a terrible thing. It can change a man into what his twisted mind is telling him he is, keeping him from knowing the power of a true identity in Christ.

The day that man terrorized the church and attempted to pin its people inside with his truck, something quiet but truly amazing happened. When brave men responded by setting their fears aside, when they took a stand against evil and stepped out of their pews, they were rewarded—not with trophies or medals but with a strengthening of their courage. They also found purpose, something bigger than themselves they were willing to die for. And the others who were present that day had their spines stiffened as they witnessed these godly men stare death in the eye, put their own safety at risk, push open the doors of fear that had held them, and let out a mighty roar—a ferocious roar that said loudly and clearly to the enemy,

*"IS THAT ALL YOU GOT?"*

## THE **BIG** QUESTION:

What are some fears you would be willing to conquer if you could really understand (or truly grasp) who you are in Christ?

# 6

# Come to the Waters

> You don't get wormy apples off a healthy tree, nor good apples off a diseased tree. The health of the apple tells the health of the tree. You must begin with your own life-giving lives. It's who you are, not what you say and do, that counts. Your true being brims over into true words and deeds.
>
> LUKE 6:43–45 MSG

The "Tree of Life," which Disney made the centerpiece of *The Lion King*, is the African baobab tree. It not only provides shade from the scorching sun but holds something much more valuable that sustains life when the dry season hits: water. Native to the African savanna, which is extremely dry for half the year, this tree is a symbol of life and hope in a landscape where little else can survive.

While in South Africa on safari with a couple of friends, I came upon this massive tree that dwarfed everything in its shade. The baobab is a succulent, which means that during the rainy season it absorbs and stores water in its vast trunk, enabling it to produce a nutrient-dense fruit in the dry season when all around is parched. This is how it became known as the Tree of Life. Not only does it produce nutritious fruit but it is made up of approximately 76 percent water; just under its tender bark is a spongy substance that's like the core of a watermelon. That core is what's so attractive to the African elephant, the only creature that can tear the tree open. They will drive their tusks repeatedly into the tree to get at that moist delicacy. One safari-goer actually witnessed an elephant so deep in the tree that it looked as if the tree were devouring the elephant! Africans call the tree roots "elephant toothpicks." I have personally witnessed elephants uprooting trees just to tear out a root to chew on for the water inside. They will stop at nothing to tap into the life inside a healthy tree.

Luke 6:43–45 reads, "You don't get wormy apples off a healthy tree, nor good apples off a diseased tree. The health of the apple tells the health of the tree. You must begin with your own life-giving lives. It's who you are, not what you say and do, that counts. Your true being brims over into true words and deeds" (MSG).

## Learning to Live Loved without the Mask of Performance

In my own journey to discover my true identity in Christ, that passage from Luke was one of the most sustaining, powerful, transformational passages I read, especially the part that says, "It's who you are, not what you say and do, that counts." For most of my childhood into adulthood, I tried to perform for my worth and value. It was all about what I said and did, or didn't do. I wasn't a popular high school athlete; I was a skinny kid who played trumpet in the back row of the band, more concerned with blending in than standing out. After high school, I worked in a Triumph motorcycle shop and a steel mill, trying to prove my masculinity and discover my purpose. Because I was always trying to prove that I was cool or tough enough, I wasn't tapping into my core and drawing from my God-given gifts and talents. My true potential, which comes from Christ *in* me, was limited because I was trying to earn my "good enough" from an external source—by how I performed and what others thought of me. I learned to put on elaborate masks that varied depending on the crowd I was hanging with. The sad part is that some of the masks worked for me; they got me what I wanted. Unfortunately, people only got to know the mask and not the real me, and as a result, I never felt good enough just the way God made me. I was left with unhealthy emotions, feeling worthless and wanting to quit if things got too hard.

My stepdaughter, Emma (my wife, Stacy, and I each have an Emma), recently went through a difficult time. She is cute as a button, is a talented little actress, and has an amazing singing voice. A local civic theater was holding auditions for *The Lion King Jr.* Emma had landed the role of Marie in their recent performance of *The Aristocats* and had gotten a taste of the fame and applause of playing a main character. Each night at the end of the show, the participants would gather at the front of the stage, take their bows to thunderous applause, and then pose for pictures and receive flowers and praise. Fame can be addictive when you don't understand the true source of your worth and value.

Before *The Lion King Jr.* auditions, Emma had her heart set on one of the lead characters, and she just *knew* she would be given the role. She practiced her singing daily and memorized not just the lines of that particular character but most of the script for the entire play. The auditions were long, with some children being called back during the day, and she was one of the callbacks. She was certain she'd won the role.

When the day came for the cast selections to be posted, Emma was confident and excited. She woke up that morning and shot out of bed, *so* eager to hear the news that she'd gotten the part. When Stacy opened the cast posting, she searched for Emma's name but couldn't find it. Finally she did. Emma had not been chosen for a lead part; she would be one of the voices in the children's chorus backing up the main characters.

When we called Emma into the room to tell her the news, she came running, full of joy, her face lit up like a sunny morning. This was going to be hard. When Stacy broke the news, her expression changed from one of joy to one of absolute heartbreak. It's a look any parent hates to see: the look of crushed

hopes and dreams. Huge tears began to flow, with a cry so painful it was as if a loved one had passed. Within a minute, her
tears turned into a storm of anger. "If I don't have a lead part,
I don't want *any* part! I didn't want to be in that stupid play,
anyway!" Emma declared. "I HATE *The Lion King*! I don't ever
want to be in another play again—EVER!"

At first we tried to comfort her, then when the anger set in,
we tried to calm her down. But it wasn't working. This was a
big blow to her self-esteem.

Several months prior, I'd had the honor, along with her
mother, to lead Emma and her sister, Sophie, to Christ and was
privileged to baptize them both. Before either of them accepted
Christ, we had many talks about what happens the moment
you truly believe, ask God to forgive you for your sins, and
ask Christ to be your Savior and Lord. We talked about how
"Christ in you" becomes your true identity, as His Spirit comes
into your spirit and gives you a new identity in Him. We talked
about how the old belief system was based on needing to *do*
good in order to *be* good, but now, because Christ is in you, you
do good because you *are* good. You no longer have to perform
or have others' good opinions for your worth and value. The
only One whose opinion matters is God, and because of that
truth, you no longer have to walk in fear but instead can walk
in total peace and confidence.

At first, I tried to help Emma understand how that applied
in this situation, but it wasn't connecting. She truly believed
that her worth and value were coming from landing that part,

because having it would mean she was someone special. Then I tried explaining to her that we don't always get what we want, and it's okay if she didn't always get the lead. That didn't help either.

I finally realized I needed to ask questions instead of trying to fix her. I asked, "If you didn't need the other kids, the director, or your parents to think you were someone special, would it bother you so much that you didn't get a lead part?" At first, with tears still rolling down her cheeks, she gave an emphatic, "Yes!" Now, that's a hard concept to understand, even for adults, so I reframed the question: "If how deeply you are loved *didn't* come from what others thought about you, about your acting or singing abilities, but because you're special just the way you are, would you still be as upset?" Then, as her crying began to subside, a peace came over her. There were still a few tears and she still wanted the part, but as her mother held her tight, she began to feel the depth of a parent's love and sank deeply into the arms of someone who loved her no matter what.

Emma made the decision to follow through with her commitment to be in *The Lion King Jr.*, singing in the chorus of more than a hundred children. After only a couple of rehearsals, there was joy on her face as she headed into each practice, and when the last light of the final performance dimmed, she'd discovered the satisfaction and purpose of being part of a team. Emma was more at peace, had a new confidence and joy, and auditioned for a role in *Peter Pan* only a few days later.

⏪◀◀◀▶▶▶⏩

One of the most painful scenes from *The Lion King* is when Scar, Simba's creepy, lying uncle, tells Simba he must run away and never come back after King Mufasa, Simba's father, is killed. Scar put together a plan to have Mufasa killed and then blame it on Simba, because Scar wants to be king. The only way he can do so is to have Simba, the rightful heir to the throne, out of the way. Scar doesn't tell the others what has happened because he knows they would never blame Simba. The truth is that Mufasa gave his life so his child might be spared. But Scar knows that if he can put the blame in Simba's mind, those lies will create unhealthy thoughts and plant shame, fear, and condemnation into Simba's heart. He knows a condemned heart will run far away, deep into isolation and hiding, and create a false self to cover up what he believes is true about himself, leaving his true purpose behind. Shame is a silent killer.

Luckily, the story doesn't end there. While Simba is roaming the plains, broken and ashamed, he runs into Pumbaa and Timon, a couple of carefree characters at the local water hole. They can tell Simba is depressed, and Pumbaa asks what's eating him. Timon jokes, "Nothing—he's at the top of the food chain!" When Simba begins to leave, Timon asks him where he's from. With his head and eyes low, Simba replies, "Who cares? I can't go back." Wanting to get into his world, Pumbaa asks, "What'd you do, kid?" Simba turns away as he answers, "Something terrible; I don't want to talk about it."

When Pumbaa asks Simba if there's anything they can do, Simba's response is profound: "Not unless you can change my past."[1]

The enemy of our souls knows that if he can keep us in past or future thinking, he's got us. Past thinking creates regret and shame and drives us into hiding, while future thoughts plant fear, worry, and doubt and give us a bad case of the what-ifs— what if I lose my car, my job, my marriage, my health, and so on?

Pumbaa and Timon teach Simba one of the most important lessons in the movie: "You've got to put your past in your behind." They teach Simba a simple song that instructs him to leave his worries and struggles in the rearview mirror, and this becomes a part of Simba's belief system, encouraging him to compartmentalize his problems. At first the song works for Simba. But trying to convince himself that he has no worries or problems isn't going to change how he feels. The problem with this philosophy is that as much as he tries to cover up what happened, it's still there. He can't bury it deep enough or make it go away by singing a catchy little tune, wishing it away, or compartmentalizing his pain. Plus, when he buries his shame so deep, his true identity gets buried as well. Simba is the rightful king, but can never become who he was born to be as long as he's running from who he really is.

Eventually, Simba can no longer carry the weight of his shame. The behavior modification, singing this "no worries" ditty over and over, is no longer working. Simba walks under a night sky, sulking in his shame, believing he is weak and without purpose and courage—that he is who the lies have told him he is. Then in walks a crazy baboon.

> SIMBA: Who are you?
>
> RAFIKI: The question is, who are you?
>
> SIMBA: I thought I knew. Now I'm not so sure.

After the crazy baboon teases Simba for a few moments, Simba tells the baboon, "I think you're a little confused." Rafiki's response hits the nail on the head, and so does his staff as he whacks Simba to wake him from the lies he's been buying into.

> RAFIKI: Wrong! I'm not the one who's confused. You don't even know who you are!
>
> SIMBA: Oh, and I suppose you know.
>
> RAFIKI: Sure do—you're Mufasa's boy. 'Bye!
>
> SIMBA: Hey! Wait! You knew my father?
>
> RAFIKI: Correction—I *know* your father.
>
> SIMBA: I hate to tell you this, but he died a long time ago.
>
> RAFIKI: Nope! Wrong again! He's alive, and I'll show him to you. You follow old Rafiki—he knows the way. Come on! Don't dawdle—hurry up!
>
> SIMBA: Hey—whoa—wait! Wait!

RAFIKI: Come on! Come on!

SIMBA: Would you slow down?

RAFIKI: Stop! Look down there. (Rafiki shows Simba his reflection in a pool of water)

SIMBA: That's not my father. That's just my reflection.

RAFIKI: No. Look harder. You see? He lives in you.

MUFASA: Simbaaaaa (a voice from the heavens speaks to Simba)

SIMBA: Father?

MUFASA: Simba, you have forgotten me.

SIMBA: No! How could I?

MUFASA: You have forgotten who you are. You have forgotten who you are, and so have forgotten me. Look inside yourself, Simba. You are more than what you have become. You must take your place in the circle of life.

SIMBA: How can I go back? I'm not who I used to be.

MUFASA: Remember who you are. You are my son, and the one true king. Remember who you are.[2]

Whether it is intentional or not, the message of the gospel in that scene cannot be missed. First Peter 2:9 tells us that we as believers are "a chosen people, a royal priesthood, a holy nation," a people belonging to God, so that we "may declare the praises of him who called [us] out of darkness into his wonderful light." Because we bear the image of the Almighty God through the blood of Jesus Christ, we not only belong to God but Christ is in us! We have His righteousness!

> But now apart from the law the righteousness of God has been made known, to which the Law and the Prophets testify. This righteousness is given through faith in Jesus Christ to all who believe. There is no difference between Jew and Gentile, for all have sinned and fall short of the glory of God, and all are justified freely by his grace through the redemption that came by Christ Jesus. God presented Christ as a sacrifice of atonement, through the shedding of his blood—to be received by faith. He did this to demonstrate his righteousness, because in his forbearance he had left the sins committed beforehand unpunished—he did it to demonstrate his righteousness at the present time, so as to be just and the one who justifies those who have faith in Jesus. (Rom. 3:21–26)

Scar led Simba into a trap and convinced him that his identity was shaped by his past. Rafiki, like the Holy Spirit, was sent to remind Simba of who he truly was, to tell him to walk boldly and confidently, and to take his rightful place because of his royal bloodline—to fulfill his purpose. All Simba had to do was believe.

Our confidence cannot come from believing in our abilities or performance or in others' opinions. Satan will shove his shame-coated lies down our throats and attempt to rob us of the confidence we have in Christ. If our confidence doesn't resonate from our core, the place where the One who conquered sin and death resides, we will fall victim to needing to appear popular, talented, gifted, or holy, and we will forever be stuck on the wheel of performance.

## Where Are Your Roots Planted?

Confidence isn't rooted in pride. It's not walking into a room thinking you're better than everyone else. **Confidence is walking into a room knowing you don't have to compare yourself to anyone else.** That only happens when we understand who God is and who He says we are. When our root systems are so shallow that we try to draw life from others instead of drawing from the living well that will never run dry, our roots remain underdeveloped and we bear unhealthy, diseased fruit. This fruit is rotten at the core because it's not drawing its sustenance from the Giver of Life but from a self-serving, works-based mentality. It is dry, shriveled fruit, sprouted from the father of lies and woven into our sin nature. Like Simba, until we can see the reflection of the Father in us, we will remain dead on the vine . . . spiritually dehydrated . . . useless.

The Father's love is a well that will never run dry and a safe place where we are washed clean by the blood of Jesus Christ. We need to come to the waters.

## Come to the Waters

*Verse 1*
Come, you who are thirsty, come to the waters
Draw from the living well—new life He offers
It's clear as crystal flowing down from the throne of
    God
Come, you who are thirsty, come to the waters

*Chorus*
Come to the well that will never run dry
Jesus alone can satisfy
All those who hear are welcome,
The Spirit and the bride say come
Come, you who are thirsty, come to the waters

*Verse 2*
Come, you who are weary, come to the waters
He leadeth me beside quiet waters
He guides me in His righteousness, He restores my
    soul
Come, you who are weary, come to the waters

*Bridge*
There's a wellspring of new life He gives
To everyone who will believe in Him
Come to the river of life
Be washed clean by the blood of Jesus Christ

          (words and music by Brent Alan Henderson)

## THE **BIG** QUESTION:

Timon and Pumbaa teach Simba to leave his worries
and struggles in the rearview mirror, encouraging him to
compartmentalize his problems. The truth is, if we *bury* it,
we *carry* it. Where do you find yourself running from your
problems, believing that somehow, by ignoring them, you
can make your struggles go away?

# The Big Five Man-Killers #2

## DISRESPECT

### *(Lion)*

Throughout history, lions have been revered as the king of the beasts. Their flowing mane, crossed forelegs as they rest without fear, four-inch canines that can crush bones in an instant, muscle power that can rip meat from hide with one swipe, and haunting stare that can paralyze prey make these beasts the most respected animal on the African continent. Lions are territorial animals that do not take disrespect lightly. And they are not just powerful; they're also very smart.

I've spent time on the African plains; you can find yourself on the menu if you don't respect the hierarchy of the food chain. In 2006, I was driving a Jeep through Kruger National Park in South Africa. At the entrance to the tent camping area where I'd spend the night, there was a high gate with a sign beside it: PLEASE CLOSE GATE QUICKLY. Near the gate was another sign: NO LOITERING. After opening the gate and driving the Jeep through, I'd stepped out to close the gate when my cell phone rang. I stood beside the open gate for several minutes talking on the phone before a park ranger came speeding up to the gate and yelled, "Do you not see the sign? Shut the gate!" At first, I was a little miffed at his attitude—how dare he speak to me that way? I responded with a little attitude of my own, "Is there a problem here?" The ranger raised his voice. "Yeah, there's a problem. Shut the gate!" Before I could say another word, the ranger leaped out of his vehicle, pulled me out of the way, and quickly closed the ten-foot-high gate. Thinking this ranger was either having a bad day or there was more to this story, I ended my call and asked if I'd done something wrong. I can still remember my shock at his reply. "There's a reason that gate has to remain shut. Lions are very smart—they've learned that this is a spot where people stop and get out of their vehicles. Just two days ago, I got out to shut the gate after pulling through, and right there in the grass a lioness was waiting, ready to pounce if I made one mistake. So when the sign says, 'Close the gate quickly,' and 'No loitering,' that's what it means!"

But as smart as lions are, they can also make mistakes when they put too much stake in their strength and intelligence. I watched a video of a young male lion who had gone out alone to explore a new territory. Not realizing where he was, he stumbled into a cackle of more than twenty hyenas. Now, a lion can take a hyena down with one paw and snap its neck like you'd snap a chicken wing. The lion disregarded the first few hyenas as they came closer, but as more ventured into his personal space, rather than leave to fight another day, his pride became his downfall. The hyenas began their cackling or "laughing" sounds. They don't do this because they're amused; a hyena's "laughter" is actually a form of communication that happens when they feel frustration, excitement, or fear. The more the hyenas laughed, the more irritated the lion became. The young, inexperienced lion got himself in trouble by trying to make the hyenas respect his size and strength. When the hyenas disrespected the lion by surrounding him and laughing excitedly, it became too much for the lion and it was game on. Before long, the group of hyenas had totally surrounded the lion and were taking turns biting him, as he couldn't control so many at once.

This is very similar to what happens when a man senses disrespect in comments made by his boss, coworkers, wife, children, and so on. Each comment by itself may be small, but when they all pile up he begins to feel devalued or backed into a corner, and, like a wild animal, will forcefully attempt to defend himself. If he wasn't mentored by his father, grandfather, uncle, or another significant male in his life, he will find himself getting into battles he's never been taught how to fight; he won't know how to defuse a tense situation and disarm those whom he perceives are attacking him. Just like the young lion, he needs the wisdom and comradeship of an older male.

Luckily, just before the hyenas could completely overtake him, another male lion heard the commotion and came to investigate, and he rescued the lone male. A cackle of hyenas might take on one male lion, but two is one too many. The healthier, wiser lion had the weaker lion's back.

When I was volunteering at a juvenile facility in central Indiana, I was brought in to speak and play some music for a group of about twenty-five troubled teen males. I felt intimidated, as I had just watched them mock the man who spoke before me. It was obvious that their comments and laughing had really thrown him for a loop; he got so flustered he couldn't remember what he was saying, finished his speech early, and left the platform visibly shaken.

As I took the stage, I had some of the volunteers pass out the printed lyrics to the song I was going to sing. As the sheets were being passed out, the teens were still laughing at how they'd shaken that other adult into quitting early, and I was about to be their next victim. But I'm sure that what I said first threw a wrench into their game plan. "Guys, I want you to know something right off the bat. I don't need your respect, and if I did, I'd have no reason to be here. I don't answer to you, I don't need you, and I don't need your approval. My worth and value have nothing to do with what you think about me. I only need the approval of the One who made everything there is, and He loved me so much that He took the bullet for me. You can listen to me or not. That's your choice."

Strangely enough, you could have heard a pin drop. After speaking to them about the song I'd written, which was about

a fatherless boy who found himself behind bars, I strapped on
my guitar and sang.

> He was eighteen years of age by the time he was ten,
> Dealing crack, headed for the pen.
> A hired hand trying for it all,
> On the other side of town where the dealer takes it all
>
> He's going down—he's headed for a fall.
>
> From a broken family, where boy meets girl, then
>     walks off free.
> Well, the boy got busted; true, but sad.
> Just another case of a boy gone bad.
> Just another case—a boy really needs a dad.
>
> Headed for a fall, trying for it all.
> Back against the wall, he's headed for a fall
>
> The boy looked down, down, down in his cell,
> And there before his eyes was the beast of hell.
> He said, "My son, my son, my son, you've done so well.
> You've led a thousand boys to a fiery well.
> A thousand screaming boys—straight to the pits of hell."
>
> Well the boy looked up and to his surprise
> There stood another Man with love in His eyes.
> The Man said, "I died for you long ago.
> There's no more debt to pay, no one to owe.
> There's no more debt to pay, cause My love has made
>     you whole!"

Headed for a fall, trying for it all.
Back against a wall—but Jesus paid it all!

(words and music by
Brent Alan Henderson)

When the song was over, there was no laughing, no jeering—
just a roomful of boys looking down and the sounds of muffled
sniffles as they tried to hold back tears, attempting to keep up
their "tough guy" façade. There was one teen I'd noticed whose
head had been down the entire time. He'd been brought in late,
accompanied by a corrections officer on either side. As the guys
were being escorted back to their rooms, this one walked by,
and I asked him what he heard me say through the lyrics of the
song. "Man, I really didn't hear much because they brought me
in late," he said. I asked why he was brought in late. "I got into
a fight with another dude because he totally dissed me—and
I don't let anyone diss me, man." I asked this tough guy one
question: "If you didn't need this dude's respect, would you
have needed to get into the fight?" He was totally bewildered.
"Huh?" I asked again. "If you didn't *need* this guy to respect
you—if your worth and value didn't come from him—would
you have needed to get into the fight?" After a couple of seconds, this tough kid's glare softened and curiosity dawned as
he replied, "No, I guess not, but . . . *how do you do that*?" Good
question.

Many of us remember the hit song "Respect," sung by Aretha
Franklin in 1967. This song became a driving force of the wom-

en's movement of the late 1960s. But did you know that song was originally released by Otis Redding in 1965, two years before Aretha ever sang it?[1] Otis penned the song as a cry to his wife, telling her that what he desperately needed from her was her respect. How difficult it would be to know that you had written a song wanting your woman to know how deeply you desired her respect only to have a woman take your song, tweak it to meet her needs, and have it become one of the most popular songs of a women's movement!

If you find yourself needing a woman's R-E-S-P-E-C-T to feel good about yourself, and what you're getting is her D-I-S-R-E-S-P-E-C-T, you might want to call your doctor right now and ask him to put you on a heavy dose of antidepressants. Giving a woman or anyone else that kind of power over you holds you captive to their opinions on any given day.

Men don't struggle with respect—they struggle with their *need* for it. They think that if they are given the respect they believe they need and deserve, then the answer to *Do I have what it takes?* will be a resounding *yes*! But when a man feels disrespected, he feels like he's just had his shorts dropped in front of his whole gym class, like his shortcomings have been exposed. The message of the arrow that just hit him is, *You're not good enough.*

Feeling disrespected is the spark that ignites the flame that lights the fuse that sets off the fireworks if it isn't trampled out immediately. When a man doesn't know where his one true identity comes from, the smallest thing can strike that match.

For many, it happens if his wife speaks to or treats him disrespectfully. He asks, "Honey, have you seen the ibuprofen?" She responds, with obvious irritation, "Have you even looked for them yet? Probably not—they're probably right in front of your face where I always find them." That might seem small, but for a man, being spoken to disrespectfully can be a trigger you don't want to pull back—his anger can be cocked, locked, and ready to rock if she's made a habit of speaking to him that way.

When a man understands that his "good enough" doesn't come from his wife speaking to him with respect, instead of reacting in anger, he can choose to respond with something disarming like, "You're probably right—I can be horrible at seeing things that are right in front of my face. I'm so glad I have your gorgeous eyes to help this blind old man!" Responding in such a way could help her see how disrespectful she's being—and even if it doesn't help, it's sure not going to hurt, right? There's a better chance that her respect will increase if her husband doesn't return her disrespect. Both may find themselves laughing instead of arguing.

There is no question that wives are instructed in Scripture to respect their husbands, but men can't control that. If you're a man who has attempted that feat, let me ask: How's that working for you? The more a man thinks he *must* have respect to be okay with himself, the more he will try to control others to get what he wants or believes he deserves. And the more he tries to force others to respect him, the less he will actually be respected. When you tell a child, "Don't touch that stove," what's the first thing that child wants to do? Touch the stove! In any relationship, if a man tries to force others to be respectful to him, do they respect him more?

We know that when a man feels respected, he feels encouraged. He feels like he has true worth. It's when respect becomes an idol to him that it conflicts with God who is in him. Until that's settled, he will struggle with anger every time he feels disrespected.

So, what is the solution to our problem with respect? The simple answer is to not need it! As long as your worth and value are connected to your desperate need for respect, you're going to be stuck on the hamster wheel of performance. **It's only when you embrace that your worth and value come from your identity in Christ and you are already good enough because the God of the universe is in you that you are free.** When that light goes on, the chains of needing others' respect fall off. You can step out from behind the bars that have been holding you captive and finally live your life free to be who God created you to be!

## THE **BIG** QUESTION:

What lies are you believing that keep you bound to needing others' respect in order to feel good enough?

# 8 From Bald Spots to Blind Spots

If growing my hair out like Samson would give me all the strength in the world, I'd probably still shave my head because I worry too much about others seeing my bald spots.

One morning while we were having breakfast, my young stepdaughter said, "Hey, I can see your hair growing out! Why don't you let it grow?" For those of you who don't know me: I'm bald, and have been for quite a while. I once had a full head of hair—down to my shoulders at one point—but the older I got, the thinner it got on top and the bigger my bald spot became. Years ago I would stand in front of the mirror and try to imagine what I would look like bald, but I just couldn't take the plunge.

Then one blustery day, I was at the Indiana State Fair with my daughter, Emma, when a kid reached up and grabbed a flap of my hair, which was coated in hairspray and blowing in the wind the way a sail does as it catches an ocean breeze. I turned around to see who had grabbed my flap, and there was a curious young boy who had been watching that flap fly up and settle back down. Up and down.

As I turned to him, he asked, "Hey, mister, why does your hair feel like cotton candy?" I'm sure his mother wanted to crawl into a hole, but he was just calling it like he saw it. My daughter and I both laughed, but inside I felt humiliated, even disrespected. I went home that day and cut off all my hair. Covering up my bald spot for so many years, worried what others might think of me, had kept me from the freedom of being okay with living with my bald spot or shaving my head. That was almost a decade ago.

We have all made choices in our lives that were influenced by what we thought others' opinions of us would be. Sometimes those influences work for our good, but other times they lead us to make choices that cause us to lose our real selves because we think we're not good enough the way we are.

I've been studying Samson. Samson's secret was his hair; as long as he didn't cut his hair, he had superhuman strength. Pondering Samson's story, I realized, *If growing my hair out like Samson would give me all the strength in the world, I'd probably* still *shave my head because I worry too much about others seeing my bald spots.*

I like me bald. I wish I would have liked me with bald spots. Loving myself just the way God created me is a part of understanding and embracing my true identity. My strength flows from the Father, not from my hair or having the respect of others. You may still have great hair, but we all have bald spots we keep trying to cover.

Ever since I was the ninety-eight-pound "wimpy kid," I've been drawn to the story of Samson. He seemed fearless. He was strong and respected, and women were drawn to him. Don't most men long for a woman to respect them and find them attractive? That was Samson's Achilles' heel.

## The Story of Samson

The life of Samson is recorded in Judges 13–16. It's the stuff of legends. When Samson got involved with Delilah, he never imagined she would be his downfall. His strength was famous throughout the land—no man could match him. Samson's story is one of great victory on one hand and incredible tragedy on the other. His purpose was to accomplish the will of God, which he ultimately did, but he also failed miserably.

Judges 13:2–14 conveys the events surrounding his birth. Before Samson's mother conceived him, she was barren. An angel appeared to her and told her that she would conceive and bear a son and that he would be a Nazirite (consecrated to God) from the womb. The Nazirite vow (see Num. 6:1–21) required a man not cut his hair for the period of the vow. Samson was a lifelong Nazirite; a razor never touched his head. Now, contrary to popular belief, Delilah was not Samson's wife. Here is the story of Samson's marriage:

> Samson went down to Timnah and saw there a young Philistine woman. When he returned, he said to his father and mother, "I have seen a Philistine woman in Timnah; now get her for me as my wife."
>
> His father and mother replied, "Isn't there an acceptable woman among your relatives or among all our people? Must you go to the uncircumcised Philistines to get a wife?"
>
> But Samson said to his father, "Get her for me. She's the right one for me." (His parents did not know that this was from the LORD, who was seeking an occasion to confront the Philistines; for at that time they were ruling over Israel.) (Judg. 14:1–4)

Can you imagine just *seeing* a woman, especially a foreigner, and then not just asking but *commanding* your dad to go get her for you? Talk about nerve—this guy definitely has some chutzpah!

Anyway, Samson and his parents head to Timnah to get his future bride. When Samson is alone, a young lion comes roaring through the vineyards toward him. What does he do? He tears it apart—not with a nine-inch sheath knife or a .458 Magnum but with his bare hands! This is one *baaaad* dude! Most men would have been bragging to everyone about what they'd done, taking selfies and posting them on social media—but Samson tells no one, not even his parents. Craving the approval of others was not an issue with Samson—at least, not yet.

At this point, Samson finally goes and actually talks to the woman he saw, and he likes her. When he returns to marry her, he passes the lion's carcass and sees a swarm of bees inside it. Me and bees? Negative. But Samson? He reaches right through the bees, scoops out a handful of honey, and eats it as he heads on his merry way. He doesn't just get a little on his fingers—he takes enough to share with his parents . . . and even then, he doesn't tell them the honey came from a lion he had torn apart with his bare hands.

> Now his father went down to see the woman. And there Samson held a feast, as was customary for young men. When the people saw him, they chose thirty men to be his companions.
>
> "Let me tell you a riddle," Samson said to them. "If you can give me the answer within the seven days of the feast, I will give you thirty linen garments and thirty sets of clothes. If you can't tell me the answer, you must give me thirty linen garments and thirty sets of clothes."
>
> "Tell us your riddle," they said. "Let's hear it."
>
> He replied,
>
>> "Out of the eater, something to eat;
>>     out of the strong, something sweet."
>
> For three days they could not give the answer.
>
> On the fourth day, they said to Samson's wife, "Coax your husband into explaining the riddle for us, or we will burn you

and your father's household to death. Did you invite us here
to steal our property?" (vv. 10–15)

"Burn you and your father's household to death"? Seriously?
These guys are worse than a drug cartel! Samson's riddle doesn't
just go over like a lead balloon—it explodes.

> Then Samson's wife threw herself on him, sobbing, "You hate
> me! You don't really love me. You've given my people a riddle,
> but you haven't told me the answer."
> "I haven't even explained it to my father or mother," he re-
> plied, "so why should I explain it to you?" She cried the whole
> seven days of the feast. So on the seventh day he finally told
> her, because she continued to press him. She in turn explained
> the riddle to her people. (vv. 16–17)

Samson is man enough to kill a lion with his bare hands, but
he caves after his wife cries for a few days! Remember when I said
problems occur when a man believes his purpose, his identity, his
"good enough" comes from what he does or what others think
of him? That belief leads a man to take his question of, *Do I have
what it takes?* to the wrong place, and if he's disrespected, it will
add fuel to his fire. Where does Samson go with his question?
To a daughter of the Philistines—and she plays him like a fiddle.

> Before sunset on the seventh day the men of the town said
> to him,

> "What is sweeter than honey?
>     What is stronger than a lion?"

Samson said to them,

> "If you had not plowed with my heifer,
>     you would not have solved my riddle."

Then the Spirit of the LORD came powerfully upon him. He went down to Ashkelon, struck down thirty of their men, stripped them of everything and gave their clothes to those who had explained the riddle. Burning with anger, he returned to his father's home. And Samson's wife was given to one of his companions who had attended him at the feast. (vv. 18–20)

Not exactly your typical wedding and honeymoon, right? But there is one thing about this that's *totally* typical, and that is the man caring too much about how he looks in front of a woman. Men buy into lies every day, striving to get their worth and value from women, other men, competition, sports, jobs, money, titles, looks, performance, and so on. When we're striving after what we think we have to have in order to feel good about ourselves, we will do really stupid things.

You'd think Samson would stay away from Philistine women after this, right? Not so. Samson then falls for Delilah, a woman from the Valley of Sorek. This marks the beginning of his demise. You see, Samson was judge over Israel at the time and had been taking great vengeance on the Philistines. It doesn't take long for the rich and powerful Philistine rulers to learn of their relationship and pay a visit to Delilah.

> Some time later, he fell in love with a woman in the Valley of Sorek whose name was Delilah. The rulers of the Philistines went to her and said, "See if you can lure him into showing you the secret of his great strength and how we can overpower him so we may tie him up and subdue him. Each one of us will give you eleven hundred shekels of silver."
>
> So Delilah said to Samson, "Tell me the secret of your great strength and how you can be tied up and subdued." (16:4–6)

Samson can silence the lion's roar with his bare hands, kill a thousand men with the jawbone of a donkey, and break any bonds put upon him, and as long as he keeps his hair, his superhuman strength will remain. The problem is that his core, his inner self, his "roar within" is silenced by the charms and tears— the seduction—of a manipulative woman.

Delilah wears Samson down, nagging him over and over (this feels much like waterboarding to a man). And then comes the "you don't really love me" Jedi mind trick. In a critical moment, he forgets where his true strength comes from, and he hands it over to her. When Samson tells Delilah that his strength would leave him if a razor were to be used on his head, she crafts a plan with the Philistine rulers. While Samson sleeps on her lap, Delilah calls in a cohort to shave off the seven braids of his hair. She had found Superman's kryptonite. In his now weakened state, he can no longer fight back and is taken prisoner . . . signed, sealed, and delivered right into the hands of the evil horde.

The Philistines decide that, rather than kill him, a more glorious revenge would be to humiliate him by gouging out his eyes and making him do hard labor. Talk about disrespect! As he slaves away at grinding grain, blinded and weak, something begins to happen: his hair begins to grow, and no one notices. And all these trials, bad choices, and sins have turned Samson's heart to the Lord. Humbled, he finally relies on God for his strength. This time, he prays to God first instead of taking matters into his own hands.

If you've ever watched the movie *Gladiator*, you can draw a parallel between the movie's main character, Maximus, and Samson. Both men have been humiliated, beaten, and tortured. Why? Because they are a threat to those who want power, and they both have something inside that is contagious to the onlookers: the power of *identity*. It is the driving force behind who they are.

In one of the most moving scenes in the movie, Maximus, once Rome's most famous general, is forced to fight to the death in the arena. Maximus's face has been concealed by a bronze galea (battle helmet). Commodus, the illegitimate emperor, calls him "slave" and commands him to remove his helmet and reveal his identity. The intensity builds as Maximus takes off his war helmet, turns around, and delivers the most memorable speech of the film: "My name is Maximus Decimus Meridius, commander of the Armies of the North, General of the Felix Legions, loyal servant to the true emperor, Marcus Aurelius, father to a murdered son, husband to a murdered wife. And I will have my vengeance, in this life or the next."[1]

The crowd that filled the Roman Colosseum had been moved by Maximus's warrior spirit and strength, and his performance brought down the house as the people stood to applaud him. Samson was about to bring down the house—and I do mean bring down the house—but no one would be standing after this performance!

> Now the rulers of the Philistines assembled to offer a great sacrifice to Dagon their god and to celebrate, saying, "Our god has delivered Samson, our enemy, into our hands."
>
> When the people saw him, they praised their god, saying,
>
> > "Our god has delivered our enemy
> >     into our hands,
> > the one who laid waste our land
> >     and multiplied our slain."
>
> While they were in high spirits, they shouted, "Bring out Samson to entertain us." So they called Samson out of the prison, and he performed for them.
>
> When they stood him among the pillars, Samson said to the servant who held his hand, "Put me where I can feel the pillars that support the temple, so that I may lean against them." Now the temple was crowded with men and women; all the rulers of the Philistines were there, and on the roof were about three

thousand men and women watching Samson perform. Then Samson prayed to the LORD, "Sovereign LORD, remember me. Please, God, strengthen me just once more, and let me with one blow get revenge on the Philistines for my two eyes." Then Samson reached toward the two central pillars on which the temple stood. Bracing himself against them, his right hand on the one and his left hand on the other, Samson said, "Let me die with the Philistines!" Then he pushed with all his might, and down came the temple on the rulers and all the people in it. Thus he killed many more when he died than while he lived. (vv. 23–30)

Samson calls out to God for his strength. No longer relying on his self-sufficiency, muscle and brawn, or "true grit," he finally understands where his strength comes from. In this final, sacrificial act, Samson destroys more of his enemies than he had previously killed in all the battles of his life.

There is no doubt that Samson was a titan of a man. He's like something out of a Marvel comic book, a real-life Avenger—the "Incredible Hulk" of the Bible. In the beginning of this chapter, we talked about how the secret of Samson's strength seemed to be his hair. What we discovered was that his strength really came through the Spirit of the Lord. His hair was merely a representation of his vow to God, not the source of his power.

The lion had roared as it attacked Samson, and in the same way, something roared inside Samson that was put there—imputed to him—not earned by his own choosing or works.

His strength didn't happen just because he willed it so. It was placed there by the One who created him.

Samson's blind spots led to bald spots that led to disaster. But as always, God worked even that out for good. Losing his eyes caused Samson to see. When he humbly cried out to God, his true strength was uncovered: God in him. When God's Spirit came upon Samson, it wasn't the result of his obedience or deeds, it was God's sovereign choice. Yes, Samson toppled the pillars that day, but it was God who made him brave and gave him strength to stand, and God who destroyed his enemies.

Though he'd lost his eyes, Samson still had a voice, one that came from deep within his true being, in his spirit, where God resided—and Samson roared!

## THE **BIG** QUESTION:

Maximus's speech was powerful because he didn't need the opinions of others to determine his true inner strength. Men typically connect what they do or how others see them with who they really are. If your title and reputation were taken away tomorrow, could you say with total confidence, "I know who I really am"?

# The Pride-Full Roar

Pride is at the bottom of all great mistakes.

JOHN RUSKIN

A cloud of African dust billowed up underneath our truck tires as the driver pushed the pedal to the metal. In our rearview mirror, the animal that Africans respectfully call Black Death, a thirteen-hundred-pound Cape buffalo, was in pursuit of our three-ton, full metal jacket safari vehicle—with absolutely no fear. We were five times his weight, yet he was on a search-and-destroy mission, and I was the fool hanging out the window taking pictures in disbelief. The driver told me that a Cape buffalo with a serious attitude problem had charged and struck the vehicle just two weeks prior, causing $20,000 in damage. These jacked-up animals can unleash a brutal, even lethal onslaught on anyone or anything that ticks them off.

The owner of the safari also told me that just a few days before I'd arrived, his brother had struck a kudu with his vehicle while returning home from a wild game capture, and the over fifty-inch horns went through the windshield and killed his brother. African animals are *huge*, and one wrong move can leave you seriously injured—or dead.

I watched a video a few years ago in which a lion found itself on the wrong side of a group of Cape buffalo. Lions may be "king of the beasts," but when a herd of Cape buffalo sticks together, a lone lion can quickly find itself with a hole the size of a coffee can in its midsection, or be seeing stars as it's flung fifteen feet in the air by the buffalo's powerful horns. When lions hunt with the pride, they outnumber the buffalo and are amazing, effective hunters. When a lion hunts without the pride, its pride can put it in a world of hurt that can leave it wounded or turn it into skin and bones rotting in the African sun.

## Pride Can Kill You

In 2015, I was on an elk-hunting trip at high elevation in the mountains of Colorado. The water filtration unit I'd recently purchased had stopped working, and I'd attempted to fix it on my own but had no luck. I was afraid it was something I'd done that had caused this, and I didn't want to disclose that

I'd probably made a mistake when reassembling it. Pride kept me quiet.

We'd had strong storms for seventeen hours, and three of us had gathered ourselves and all our gear underneath two tarps until the storm passed. During those seventeen hours, I drank no water—just stayed cocooned inside my sleeping bag and bivy sac to stay dry. When the skies cleared and the rain stopped, everything we had was soaked and we needed to make the five-mile climb back to the truck—a killer hike from about 8,500 to 10,500 feet with a number of switchbacks on the journey.

I had trained incredibly hard for this trip and was feeling somewhat prideful that I was in the best shape of my life. I wanted to prove to the guys and to myself that I could keep up with these western hunters. I wanted to earn their respect. Yeah—*big* mistake. I may have been in better shape, but they had experience and understood the environment we were in. They also lived at an altitude of 6,000 feet, whereas this flat-lander has spent the majority of his life at 800 feet. This was their backyard, and they knew how quickly you can get dehydrated at high altitudes. I'd spent a lot of time in Alaska, but there in the Last Frontier things start at sea level. My flight into Colorado landed in the mile-high city of Denver, and it was all uphill from there.

Just twelve months prior, I'd almost been swept away in a canyon in the dark of night when a massive storm had flooded our camp. Its raging waters surrounded us, pushing boulders the size of Volkswagens around like marbles and tossing logs as big as telephone poles as if they were toothpicks, within just feet of our tent. Everything I owned was soaked, including the clothes on my back, and I had developed the beginning stages of hypothermia. Had the torrential rains not stopped, either the rising waters would have swallowed us whole or we all would have ended up becoming food for the coyotes, mountain lions, and black bears. Yet here I was one year later, back in the same canyon, where it had been raining cats and dogs *and* I'd messed up my water filtration system. Like they say, "You can't fix stupid."

As we began loading up for the five-mile journey out of the muddy canyon bottom, I discovered my pack hadn't made it all the way under the tarp. For seventeen hours, the rain had been soaking through it, saturating all of its contents. When I lifted my pack, I found that it now weighed more than twice what it had originally weighed—close to eighty pounds. At age twenty-five, I might have thought this seemed like a good test of my male prowess. At fifty-five, I wasn't looking for a way to become the next American Ninja Warrior.

The first mile wasn't bad—just the occasional mud hole to navigate around or a random log across our path. Then came the next four miles—all uphill. Some sections were so steep, switchbacks had been cut into the mountainside to make the climb humanly possible. Because of the sheer volume of water that had been dumped on the area, the trail had become a slippery quagmire. Thick mud stuck to our boot soles like giant flapjacks, and each step was like trying to pull a sledgehammer out of a giant tub of peanut butter. Whenever I would step to the side to bang my feet against a tree, log, or rock to dislodge the mud, the weight of my pack would cause me to start tipping sideways, and more than once I had to grab for whatever was secured to the ground to keep from tumbling down the steep mountainside.

Miles three and four were rough, but by mile five I wasn't just exhausted—I was also severely dehydrated, and the thumbs on both my hands closed shut like vise grips. When we finally arrived back at the truck, I asked my buddy, Roger, to help pry my thumbs open. Once he realized I hadn't been drinking water, he gave me some from his unit, then drove us the hour into town to a restaurant, where I downed three large glasses of water on the count of one. But it wasn't until the next morning that I realized just how bad things really were.

## Going Blind

Because everything was soaked and we were exhausted, the three of us made the decision to get a hotel for the night so we could dry out our things, get a good night's rest, and then head to camp in a new location about two hours away. While eating breakfast in the hotel restaurant, I complained that someone must have burned their waffles in the waffle iron, because the room was filling with smoke. The two men looked at me, puzzled, with the same "I think he's losing his mind" look I'd seen the year before when I was in the beginning stages of hypothermia and they'd had to threaten to take my wet clothes off and put me between the two of them inside a sleeping bag. Upset that they thought I'd lost my marbles, I got up and walked out into the hotel hallway. It was filled with smoke as well. I walked over to the hotel guest services desk and promptly asked the clerk if there was smoke in the hall. Her look let me know I was either going crazy or something was seriously wrong with me.

I quickly made my way to the stairwell and raced up the flight of stairs to our room. By the time I opened the door and looked in the mirror, it was like looking into a mirror where a hot shower had been left running for hours. By the time the other guys got to the room, I knew I was in trouble, but I thought it would pass. With some not-so-gentle convincing, they had me get on the phone with my doctor back in Indiana after they dialed the number for me. When I described to the receptionist what was happening, she didn't put a nurse on the line; she immediately went and got a doctor, who proceeded to tell me I needed to get to the emergency room ASAP. Of course, I resisted; I told the doctor that going there could be the end of the hunt for me. But the voice on the other end of the call grabbed my full attention as she said, "This could be not just the end of your hunt, but the end of your *life* if you don't go right now." All I remember after that was her using the words "possible stroke," and immediately my thoughts went to watching my father pass away after having a massive stroke just one year earlier.

As we left the hotel lobby, the only thing my eyes could detect was whether it was dark or light. Both men grabbed an arm; they got me in the truck, and off we went. Upon our arrival in the ER, a nurse placed me in front of a wall with an eye chart on it and asked me to read the smallest line I could see. My response let her know just how dire my situation was: "Ma'am, what wall?" The nurse quickly led me to a bathroom, placed a small plastic cup in my hand, and told me she needed a urine sample. Her words, "If you need help, I can help you," caused me to laugh even in my grim situation. (I got teased about that one for a while.) "Thanks for the offer, but I think I can handle that part," was my response. After taking my urine sample, they led me to a bed in the ER where I waited for my next adventure: a CT scan.

Within an hour of my tests, two doctors came to my bedside and gave me the diagnosis. My brain scan had revealed I'd had trauma to my head sometime in my past, but what was more concerning was that my urine was brown. They explained I had something called rhabdomyolysis. Rhabdomyolysis, or "rhabdo," is a degeneration of muscle cells and is characterized by muscle pain, tenderness, a locking up of the muscles, weakness, and swelling, plus myoglobinuria (the presence of myoglobin, a protein found in muscle tissue, in the urine). When blood myoglobin concentrations rise due to muscle damage and severe dehydration, and the renal threshold for filtering this protein is reached, myoglobin can spill over into the urine, coloring it with a light tinge of brown. Overloaded by the elevated levels of myoglobin, the kidneys can struggle, leading to renal failure in some severe cases. The doctors' next words were, "Sir, if we can't get this turned around within the next twenty-four hours, you'll be on dialysis."

They warned me of the seriousness of my condition, informing me that two other hunters had died from rhabdo just weeks before. Questions suddenly began exploding in my mind like popcorn: *How could this be? How did I get here? What happens if I have to go on dialysis?* Worse yet, *What if I'm blind the rest of my life? How could I ever hunt again? Heck, how could I ever do much of anything I loved?* Rhabdo may be a silent killer, but so was my need for respect that got me into this predicament. This was going to change everything in my life—for the *rest* of my life!

By the next morning nothing had changed, except I'd had more time to worry and my anxiety had increased. On the outside I was making jokes, but on the inside I was scared to death. A doctor walked into my room, sat by my bedside, and asked me my name. After I answered, he asked me if I could read his hospital name tag. I couldn't even make out the outline of his body. I needed a miracle in the next few hours, and I knew what could happen if God didn't show up in a big way.

Then the second-most excruciating pain I've ever experienced happened when the doctor proceeded to roll my eyelids up to keep them open and accidentally jammed my left eye with his thumbnail. But the *most* physical pain I've ever experienced was at a church camp as a child, when I caught my eye on the corner of a metal Ping-Pong table, which I hit at full speed while running to stop a ball from rolling under it. It took two hours to get me to the hospital; they had to do emergency surgery without putting me under anesthesia. With all that trauma, you'd think the pain would be all I'd remember, but it isn't. What I remember most had nothing to do with almost losing my eye. My biggest memory of that incident is of a man holding me in his arms the entire way to the hospital. I remember that someone held me through my pain; he stayed with me the entire journey and never left my side.

[You're not going to believe this: that man who held me, now in his seventies, just walked through the door of Panera Bread, where I sit writing this. This man lives near the camp where that injury occurred . . . *five hundred miles away* from where I sit right now. There is no doubt in my mind that God orchestrated our meeting here at this exact time.]

The doctor put some drops in my eye that were supposed to help him detect if there were any injuries to my eye. Well, if there weren't any before, there was certainly one now, thanks to his lancing me with his thumbnail! And whatever was in those drops stung worse than a probe on a nerve in an open root canal. For the next six hours, I must have pushed the pain button attached to my bed a dozen times; I've never felt anything so painful in my adult life.

By morning, through bloodshot, swollen, sleepless eyes, my eyesight had slowly begun to improve. I was able, just barely, to distinguish moving images on the TV in front of my bed. The pope was visiting the United States, and as time passed I could make out the image of him, dressed in white, standing up in a bulletproof vehicle.

It was about at that time when my friend Roger came into my hospital room after going back to the hotel for a couple of hours of sleep. "How are you this morning, sunshine?" Roger always has a way of lifting me up when things are difficult. "Aren't you about ready to quit lounging around in bed and get back to hunting elk?" Over the next few hours, my eyesight began to improve rapidly, enough so that the doctor was willing to release me to Roger's care. But he warned me very sternly not to put myself back in the position that got me there and required I schedule a meeting with an eye specialist across town before completing my full release.

After meeting with the specialist and getting the okay to leave hospital care, I cut my plastic hospital bracelet off and excitedly said to Roger, "Well, are we headed back out to see if we can find some elk to invite home for dinner?" We both laughed. Although he agreed to take me back out, he gave me some firm guidelines to make sure I wouldn't get myself in that position again, and we stuck to them. Roger wasn't going to allow me to put myself in a position where my pride and foolishness could eat me for lunch. Roger had been my armor-bearer, my friend, and my guide and had stayed closer than a brother. We all need a Roger in our lives.

## Pride Comes before a Fall

I'll say this again: confidence isn't rooted in pride. It's not walking into a room thinking you're better than everyone else. **Confidence is walking into a room knowing you don't have to compare yourself to anyone else.**

I had been one month away from my fifty-fifth birthday, was in the best shape of my life, and was feeling prideful. It's amazing how quickly things can go bad when we make poor choices. What's that old saying about pride coming before a fall? I found out it's true.

Here's a picture of me on day two of our hunt.

I was ripped, feeling prepared, and thinking I was ready to take the mountains and high altitude head-on.

Here is day four—just two days later, after messing up my hydration system and being soaked to the core, making everything I was packing out so much heavier.

And finally, pride and stupidity caught up with me, landing me in the emergency room, dangerously dehydrated and blind.

In the last picture, you can see my left eye is a little more closed than my right eye. That was a result of either the doctor gouging my eye or some nerve damage from the rhabdomyolysis.

To this day, I have to focus on lifting that eyelid, as it doesn't open
on its own as much as the opposite
eye. There are consequences when
we choose poorly.

Most of us think the first sin
was Adam and Eve's disobedience
in the Garden of Eden, resulting
in the fall. We know from Scripture that this was the first *human*
sin, but it is not the first sin found
throughout God's creation. The
serpent tempted Eve, but it was the
devil's fall from grace that set the
course for the fall of humankind. He was prideful and wanted
to have a throne higher than God's.

> You were the anointed cherub who covers;
> I established you;
> You were on the holy mountain of God;
> You walked back and forth in the midst of fiery stones.
> You were perfect in your ways from the day you were
>     created,
> Till iniquity was found in you.
>     (Ezek. 28:14–15 NKJV)

What was the first sin?

> How you are fallen from heaven,
> O Lucifer, son of the morning!
> How you are cut down to the ground,
> You who weakened the nations!
> For you have said in your heart:
> "I will ascend into heaven,
> I will exalt my throne above the stars of God;
> I will also sit on the mount of the congregation
> On the farthest sides of the north;
> I will ascend above the heights of the clouds,
> I will be like the Most High."
> Yet you shall be brought down to Sheol,
> To the lowest depths of the Pit.
>     (Isa. 14:12–15 NKJV)

Satan's sin was pride. He was so caught up in his power, wisdom, and appearance that he wanted God's position and authority. He wanted to be God. He wanted to be above all creation, to be worshiped. How different this is from Jesus, who came to bring life, to empty Himself instead of exalting Himself, to build a bridge so that all humankind could have a relationship with God and have eternal life.

What is so destructive about pride? What effect does it have on us? Pride causes us to rebel against God; to want not to serve but to be served; to not be authentic but to pose and to flaunt; to want to be admired, even worshiped. It promises recognition and respect but delivers destruction.

Do you know where the phrase "pride comes before a fall" originated? Look at these verses in Proverbs:

> Pride goes before destruction,
> And a haughty spirit before a fall. (16:18 NKJV)

> When pride comes, then comes shame;
> But with the humble is wisdom. (11:2 NKJV)

> Before destruction the heart of a man is haughty,
> And before honor is humility. (18:12 NKJV)

Unhealthy thoughts and emotions lead to sin, sin leads to shame, and shame leads us into hiding, causing us to let others see only what we want them to see (only the *best* of us), which propagates pride.

My thoughts on the mountain that day were about covering up my mistake in breaking my water filtration unit and needing to prove I was in great shape to win the respect of my friends. The beliefs that shaped those thoughts were rooted in the Big Lie: my performance + others' opinions = my self-worth. It was being so full of pride, needing to prove my physical prowess, that led me to perform in an unhealthy way because I believed I *had to have* their good opinion. And it was my buying into the Big Lie, operating out of fear of not being good enough, that almost took my life that day. Had I operated out of the truth— that my worth and value have nothing to do with how well I perform or what others think of me—it would have quieted the angry roar based in that fear. I wouldn't have put my life in jeopardy, wouldn't have ruined the hunt for my close friends, and wouldn't have risked creating substantial difficulties for loved ones who would have had to take care of me for the rest of my life if I had gone blind.

## THE **BIG** QUESTION:

The beliefs that shape our unhealthy thoughts are rooted in the Big Lie: my performance + others' opinions = my self-worth. What is the dumbest thing you've ever done to attempt to gain the respect of others? How did it work for you?

# The Big Five Man-Killers #3

## ANGER

*(Cape buffalo)*

Cape buffalo are also called "Black Death" and "widow-maker." They have killed more big-game hunters than any other animal in Africa; it is estimated that they gore and kill more than two hundred people every year.[1] A full-grown male can be almost six feet tall at the shoulder and weigh almost a ton; when this massive freight train of horn and muscle comes off the track, it will destroy anything in its path. I've watched one toss a crocodile ten feet in the air because it came after one of the herd. I was in a full metal jacket safari vehicle when one of these behemoths with a bad attitude charged our truck for simply driving past the herd. In the right circumstance, their anger can serve them well. Misguided, their anger can cause extreme damage.

In one of my "not-made-for-TV" moments over a decade ago, I found myself beating up a stack of empty cardboard boxes on the back porch after my wife spoke disrespectfully to me. I didn't know what to do with my anger and didn't want to take it out on my wife or anyone else, so those boxes bore the brunt. Then I left the demolished boxes there for her to see so she would know how upset her disrespect had made me. My unhealthy actions didn't get the response I was hoping for; I had to learn to *talk* about my emotions. Men and women both experience many emotions; they can feel sad, glad, angry, hurt, excited, afraid, and many other things. But through the masculine lens, anger is the only "difficult" emotion that is socially acceptable.

There are many social prohibitions against men expressing emotions like sadness or fear, yet men receive reinforcement for expressing anger. Society perceives men who outwardly express anger as being powerful or more masculine and men who express sadness or fear as weak or more feminine. Receiving affirmation for expressing anger can make a man feel justified and powerful when he flips that switch. But what's happening underneath the hood that sparks his anger? When a man turns that key, it's usually so he doesn't appear vulnerable or afraid. He's building a false identity, a shell to protect himself, because at his core, feeling the difficult emotions scares him to death.

In another of my "not-made-for-TV" moments, my wife and I were in Pennsylvania, and I'd just performed the ceremony for my niece's wedding. At the reception hall afterward there was an open bar, and as the evening progressed it became obvious the bartender had himself been drinking. My wife and I were standing only about ten feet away having a conversation when she started looking nervous. When I asked her what was wrong, she told me that the bartender had been staring at her inappropriately and was creeping her out. My wife is gorgeous, and she has a smile that melts me like nothing else can. I could stare at her for hours, but I'm her husband, so I'm allowed. I moved in front of her so the bartender couldn't see her anymore, and he suddenly stepped out from behind the counter and said, "Ma'am, you look so hot in that dress." Then he looked at me with a smirk and said, "I'm not trying to hit on your wife or anything." He knew he'd gotten under my skin through being disrespectful, and now *I* was getting hot! This called for an A-game response, and the words came out of my mouth faster than a major league pitch: "That's okay, because I hit back—and I hit *really hard*!" My wife looked at me with eyes that said, *Did you really just say what I think you said?* Yes, I did. And I was the pastor who'd just performed a wedding ceremony a couple of hours earlier!

There are times when anger is appropriate. If you see a person being physically abused, a child being molested, or the enemy using shame to destroy a person's life, that *should* make you angry! That's not an unhealthy anger; it's a righteous anger, driving you to protect those who are in harm's way. Jesus was both the Lion *and* the Lamb; it's important for us to know when anger is appropriate and when it's not. We need to constantly ask ourselves "WWJD?" (What would Jesus do?) To be honest, both kinds of anger were in play at that moment. It was right to be angry at a man disrespecting my wife and making her feel uncomfortable (and likely unsafe) by leering at her. It was right for me to defend her. But his disrespect of *me* also triggered my anger because of my unhealthy need for his respect.

An issue that can get under a man's skin quickly is road rage. I recently had to deal with my own anger when a $70,000 SUV was riding my bumper no more than two feet away. I was in the middle of passing three semitrucks on a two-lane highway. They were going uphill and were well below the posted speed limit. After passing the first of the three trucks, I noticed in my rearview mirror the SUV coming from behind at about 100 miles per hour. He didn't have his four-way hazard lights on indicating there was an emergency, and he wasn't waving his arms out the window or doing anything that would make me think I needed to speed up. I was already going a couple of miles per hour over the speed limit. As he practically glued himself to my back bumper, I noticed he was holding his hand up. Well, maybe not his whole hand—just one finger—and he wasn't telling me I was number one.

Now, I understand this was his issue, not mine. But there is something inside of men that, when they feel they are being disrespected, especially when they believe they've done nothing wrong, is like hearing the loudspeakers on a WWII Navy destroyer crying out, "Battle stations!" If you're not in a good place mentally and spiritually, it will create a fight-or-flight response.

Remember, it's all about identity. If I'm getting my worth and value from the wrong place, I will try to control my world to give me what I think I need to be good enough. Instantly, my flesh wanted to either step on the gas or slow down just to throw a little disrespect back in his face. For ten seconds or so, my mind wrestled with what to do. Do I hit my brakes? That could cause a massive pileup and we'd all be dead, making *me* a "widowmaker." Do I try to slide over between the semis as s-l-o-w-l-y as possible, provoking him to pull into the emergency lane to get around me more quickly? That would be putting him at risk, and even if he did seem to be angry at the whole world, that wouldn't be right. Do I flex my bicep out the window at him as he passes, insinuating, "Hey, you want a piece of this?" Do I let him know I think he's number one as well? Nope—I have to let that one go.

So, what *did* I do? I asked the Holy Spirit to help me with my *own* anger and to help me realize that whatever anger that guy had allowed to become his own, I was guilty of the same. Once I took personal responsibility for my anger, I simply got out of his way as soon as I was safely past the last semi and then repented of my own sin. It's amazing how quickly our anger can subside when we honestly examine and take responsibility for it. Who knows? Maybe my not lashing out at him enabled him to see his own anger—or not; it doesn't matter. We are all responsible only for our *own* anger and actions, and they will never be solved by "sin management." We can't fix this on our own. Only God in us can kill this man-killer.

Feeling disrespected *can* kick a man's anger into overdrive and knock his thinking off the tracks, turning him into a freight train of unhealthy actions. But when he's living out of his one true identity, he discovers that the only one whose opinion really matters is Christ. And that black death of a man's old nature that just wants to get even is replaced with love, joy, peace, patience, kindness, goodness, faithfulness, gentleness, and self-control. Living out of our identity in Christ is an anger-killer!

## THE **BIG** QUESTION:

What is something others have done that got under your skin and made you feel disrespected? Would it bother you as much if you didn't need their respect? Why or why not?

# When Bears and Opinions Attack

The sound was like two rocks grinding together as the bear drug his canines across my scalp.

BROWN BEAR ATTACK SURVIVOR

Alaska is beautiful, but it's loaded with lots of things that go bump in the night—earthquakes, tsunamis, volcanoes, glaciers, landslides, avalanches, high winds, minus-60 degree temperatures, blizzards, thirty-foot tidal changes, and more. It's full of things that can eat you for lunch, and bears are one of them. Wild bears are scary—period. They are not the well-kept, docile bears you see at the zoo, pacing back and forth in their enclosure, waiting to be fed. In the wilds, they are incredibly spooky and unpredictable, and when they're hungry, they kill.

An angry brown bear can really spoil a good day. When a brown bear is born, it weighs only about a pound, but in just six years, a male brown bear has transformed from that one-pound adorable cub into a fifteen-hundred-pound killing machine. Brown bears can reach over ten feet tall—higher than a basketball rim—with claws almost four inches long. They've been known to smash doors right off their hinges and rip through metal siding like opening a pop can. A brown bear can smell carrion, the flesh of a dead animal, from extreme distances—up to *eighteen miles away*. Almost every year there are stories of brown bear attacks and fatalities of unsuspecting "volunteers" with whom brown bears have tried to "play." I've had several encounters with them, and just thoughts of these behemoths can keep you on edge and in your cabin eating canned salmon if you let the tales get into your head.

Brown bears have a perimeter line you cannot cross, but *when* and *where* that line is can change from moment to moment. They can be tolerant of you at twenty feet or get perturbed when you're fifty yards away. I've seen them suddenly go ballistic on a lone seagull treading water fifteen feet away, patiently waiting for a morsel of pink sockeye to drift its way. They're like a ticking time bomb, and you'd better hope you're not the one who lights that fuse.

While I was filming brown bears on the Russian River in the summer of 2011, I had a male brown bear decide to draw a boundary. I'd been filming him for about ten minutes when he came out of the water onto the shore just four yards away and began moving me backward until he was satisfied with the distance. The whole time I was being pushed backward, my hand was firmly gripped around my Taurus Raging Bull .44 Magnum, and I was having a one-way conversation with him: "Hey, bear! Whoa, bear!" He didn't listen.

In July 2009, a friend and I were camped not far from a salmon hot spot near Cooper's Landing, Alaska, on the Kenai Peninsula. We'd just stowed some gear and were unpacking our sleeping bags for the night when an ambulance came flying by, sirens wailing. I looked at my friend, who cocked his eyebrows as he said, "Either there's been a wreck, or someone got hammered by a bear."

At seven the following morning, we walked across the road to the local bait shop. The owner stepped out from behind the counter, looked at us with wild eyes, and said, "Hey, did you hear a woman got mauled by a brown bear last night less than a half mile away? I guess she'd just arrived from the lower 48 to work for the summer at one of the gift shops—went out to smell the flowers about ten o'clock last night and surprised a brown bear with a really bad attitude."

Being men, of course the first thing we did was get in our truck and drive to the spot where the mauling had occurred. Walking down the path toward the site of the attack, there was a sign posted at the trailhead: "Warning! If you are hiking or backpacking into the wilderness, it's important to be on the lookout for bears. We highly recommend you wear a large jingle bell on your pack to signal to the bears you're in their area, and also carry a large canister of bear pepper spray. It is also advised that you be familiar with the difference between black bear scat and brown bear scat. Black bear scat is full of small animal fur and berry seeds, while brown bear scat is full of jingle bells and smells like pepper spray!" Great—just what I needed—more unhealthy fodder for my brain.

When we arrived at the exact spot of the attack, there was a freshly cut pile of alder bush branches covering the trail so that tourists couldn't see any remnants of the occurrence. After taking pictures of the location, the two of us went into the gift shop where the young woman had been working to try to get an interview with someone who had seen the event or had the story firsthand. The older woman behind the counter told us it had been around ten o'clock the night before when Debbie, the new summer employee, walked around the back of the shop to smell a patch of flowers. That's when it happened. For whatever reason, the spooked bear angered and instantly attacked. A man and his daughter were visiting here at the time; they said at first they just thought someone was laughing uncontrollably behind the shop, but when he went to see what was so funny, he saw the bear standing upright, holding Debbie in its mouth by her head. He immediately yelled for his daughter to call 911, and he began shouting and throwing things at the bear. The bear finally dropped her before it could shake her like a rag doll, and she was rushed by ambulance to a helicopter that life-flighted her back to Anchorage.

The gift shop worker told us that the one thing Debbie wanted to see while in Alaska was a brown bear, as she'd never seen a bear in the wilds. Well, she got her wish. We were later told that after hundreds of stitches to her scalp, she came out of surgery at 3:00 a.m., and the first thing she said to the surgeon was to ask him to call her mother and tell her she'd finally seen a bear! I'm not sure those would have been my first words.

That same afternoon, we were returning to camp with a stringer of salmon when I spotted a huge brown bear walking along the shoreline and getting ready to pass underneath the bridge we were about to drive over. My friend stopped the truck, and I grabbed my video camera, ran across the bridge, and prepared to film it, as it would pass not more than ten yards below me. Yeah, I know—I'm not the sharpest tool in the shed. The moment the bear appeared, I turned on my video camera. As the camera powered on, the shutter lens made a clicking sound as it opened up. Like I said, you never know what's going to set a bear off, and you just hope you're not the one who lights the fuse.

Before I could look into the viewfinder, the bear looked directly at me, lowered its ears flat to its head (not a good sign), and started coming up the steep embankment directly at me. There was absolutely no fear on its part. I can't say the same for myself; before I could even soil my pants, I was back on top of the bridge, running alongside a tourist driving a motorhome, his mouth gaping and his eyes the size of dinner plates. As I reached the opposite side of the bridge, my friend and I jumped back into the truck, drove straight back to the gift shop, and had them call the Alaska Department of Fish and Game. Typically, if a bear sees, hears, or smells you, it's outta there; if it doesn't leave, there's a good chance it's a rogue bear. This was likely the same bear that had attacked Debbie the night before. A short time later, a couple of game wardens showed up and dispatched it. This bear would give no more headaches.

Usually bears leave you alone, but on rare occasions they don't. I've been "woofed" at, bluff-charged, and pushed back by bears. I've gone up a tree to get away from a bear, heard them sniff my two-man tent at night, and had them tear open a tire cover on the back of a motorhome. I've walked the banks of the Russian River (which is loaded with brown bears) in the pitch-black night trying to locate a missing person. If you're going to run into a rogue bear, it's likely going to happen at night, and from what I just told you, you probably don't want to run into a bear if I'm around! Thousand-pound brown bears are on the top of my list of things in the wild that cause me fear and anxiety.

As difficult as it is to be in close proximity to brown bears (and get within feet of them when filming), there's one place where my anxiety can really cause my fight-or-flight response to activate in a hurry, but it's not a situation where a .44 Magnum can stop the problem.

## Bears Can Eat You Alive, and So Can the Opinions of Others

Several years ago, I went through a painful divorce. The Bible tells us that God hates divorce, and He does. That's not to say that there aren't situations where divorce is necessary, but it's not a clean cut—it's a ripping apart of everything you've known, hoped for, believed in, and fought for. It's a massive loss where everyone is affected. The only way I can explain the pain of divorce is when I see a brown bear tear the skin from a salmon right off the meat, sometimes tearing the fish in half, exposing ribs and guts. Divorce tears you apart—not just for a moment but for years.

One of the most difficult outcomes from divorce is that people—friends, family, those who say they love you both and are just sad it happened—will take sides. It's going to happen. The gossip wheel gets fired up, and before you know it, some of those you love will turn away. They will create their own narrative to justify their position or unhealthy actions. They may pretend they don't see you in a public place, or let you know they see you and give you the evil eye, or say they're "praying for you" in a condescending way. Just as soldiers who fought the enemy in war come back with a thousand-yard stare, those who've gone through divorce understand that it's like being in a long, bloody battle. The biggest difference is that these people weren't your enemies before, but now they treat you as if you are theirs.

Maybe I should've worn a bear bell to let them hear me coming so they could leave the room or disappear into another store aisle—that way I wouldn't have had to witness their shunning. Better yet, I could've carried an industrial-size can of bear spray so that when they gave me that judging stare I could just

. . . well, um . . . yeah . . . never mind. That was an unhealthy thought—it was vindictive, angry, and not from God. But if I'm being honest, that's where my mind was fighting to go, and I have to battle those thoughts just like anybody else. This unhealthy thought—feeling like I needed to get even—was one of those well-placed flaming arrows that does far more damage to me than it could do to my enemies.

Sometime after I remarried, Stacy and I went to see my friend and former tour partner, Steven Curtis Chapman. He was doing a solo concert at our alma mater, and a lot of people who came that night knew me and knew I'd gone through a divorce. Knowing there could be those in attendance who might give us the cold shoulder, I said to her on the way in, "We walk humbly, remember who we are in Christ, and walk with quiet confidence in Him. The only one whose opinion truly matters is God." As much as we knew that truth, I'd be lying if I didn't say it was a struggle for me to stay in that truth. Within seconds of walking into the lobby of the auditorium, I saw a group of friends, some of whom I'd known and loved for thirty years. As I approached the group, a woman who I'd thought would handle the situation with grace and love looked at me with the eyes of Medusa, and had I not been secure in my identity, I think I'd have turned to stone. Her intent was to hurt me, and for a few moments, she succeeded. As I walked up to her, ready to reach out and give her a hug, she gave me a stare of disgust, loathing, and intense anger. In that moment it felt as if she were a thousand-pound grizzly and had placed my head directly in her mouth, trying to devour me. I could smell the decaying flesh of judgment, and it felt like canines were being dragged across my cold, clammy scalp. Luckily, grizzlies can't open their mouth far enough to swallow your head whole, but they will try unless you have the right weapon and the courage to stop the onslaught. Those who shun have judgment caught in their throats—but they can't eat us unless we let them.

Why do we give others the power to make us feel angry or ashamed? Did they create us? Do they know our story? Have they walked in our shoes? Why is it that others' opinions—their judging, shaming, gossip, and shunning—bother us so much?

The way to survive a bear attack isn't to try to outrun the bear—that ain't gonna happen! You have to have the right weapon for the job and know how to use it. In the same way, you can't defeat others' judgment with judgment of your own. You can't stare down starers in hopes they will blink first. As a matter of fact, if you *have* to win, you've already lost. You need to know—you must truly understand—that it's their issue! It's *their* anger. It's *their* judgment. It's *their* sin. They are responsible for their own actions. **There is nothing we can do to fix or control how someone else acts or what they choose to believe.** Our job isn't to clean their side of the street. Our job is to keep *our own* side of the street clean. To love. To be patient. To understand they're struggling as well—and believe me, they know they are, because sin leaves a bitter taste.

Romans 14:4 and 12 are such powerful verses:

> Who are you to pass judgment on the servant of another? It is
> before his own master that he stands or falls. . . . So then each
> of us will give an account of himself to God. (ESV)

Avoiding people isn't going to solve the issue, and neither
is shaming them for their hurtful actions. Remember, they're
hurting too—that's why they're angry. So, what do we do when
we come under an attack like this? God gives us great insight
on how to handle others' judgment in Romans 12.

> Bless those who persecute you; bless and do not curse them. . . .
> Repay no one evil for evil, but give thought to do what is honor-
> able in the sight of all. If possible, so far as it depends on you, live
> peaceably with all. Beloved, never avenge yourselves, but leave it
> to the wrath of God, for it is written, "Vengeance is mine, I will
> repay," says the Lord. To the contrary, "if your enemy is hungry,
> feed him; if he is thirsty, give him something to drink. . . ." Do not
> be overcome by evil, but overcome evil with good. (vv. 14, 17–21)

Another powerful verse to remember if you are the one using
shame and condemnation toward others is Romans 2:4.

> Or do you think lightly of the riches of His kindness and toler-
> ance and patience, not knowing that the kindness of God leads
> you to repentance? (NASB)

Remember that those who've experienced the pain of divorce, addictions, and so forth are hurting too. Would shaming,

shunning, judging, or gossiping be helpful to you if you were in their shoes? Putting yourself in their place (empathy) is a powerful way to *understand* others instead of wanting to punish them, which only leaves you with a gushing wound of your own. Your judgment exposes the condition of your own heart. **It's God's kindness, tolerance, and patience that lead us to repentance.** Write that down. Put it on your rearview mirror, stick it in your wallet, get it tattooed on your head if you have to (okay—maybe just write it on your palm). Do whatever it takes to learn and weave that truth into the very core of your being.

Our response to others when they're acting in an unhealthy manner toward us reveals the condition of our own hearts. It reveals where our roots are planted: in the shallow ground of the enemy's lies or in the deep, fertile ground of God's truth. Who I am has *nothing* to do with what others think of me but everything to do with what God thinks of me. As I am a believer, God does not look at my sin or at what others think about me. He not only sees the righteousness of Christ when He looks at me but also sees the real me He created before sin came into the world—and He doesn't care about the opinions of others. His opinion is the only one that matters. *Never* forget that. That is our .44 Magnum that stops the lies of the enemy dead in their tracks. And we can choose, through Christ, to love those who persecute us.

A .44 Magnum lets out a heck of a roar when fired, but the Lion of Judah, who *lives in me*, lets out a deafening roar that resounds across the entire universe when I live out who I really am in Christ. As soon as I forget who—and whose—I am, I make myself subject to the opinions of others. My anger causes me to start judging the judgers, and that judgment silences the roar within me, gets caught in my own throat, and mutes the glory and power of Christ in me. But the roar of the righteous will stop any attack of the enemy and be a sobering reminder to those who hear and witness it that God is King and is seated on His throne.

ROAR, my believing friends, for at your core is the righteousness of Christ!

## THE **BIG** QUESTION:

Whenever we allow others' opinions of us to determine our self-worth, we give them power to make us feel resentful and "less than." To whom have you given power, allowing their opinions to determine your perceived worth and value?

# 12

# Quieting the Angry Roar

Fear has one of two meanings:
**F**orget **E**verything **A**nd **R**un
or
**F**ace **E**verything **A**nd **R**ise.
You get to choose.

A voice rang out from the huge 4x4 passing me to my left. "Get off your d@^^ phone!" As I turned to look toward the sound of the outburst, I saw a twenty-something male glaring at me. His hat was spun around backward, his thin, unshaven beard extended down his neckline, and his bottom lip protruded from an oversized wad of chewing tobacco. And there was no doubt what he was trying to say as he repeatedly thrust his middle finger at me.

It was rush hour in downtown Indianapolis, and I was using my phone's GPS. The passenger in the elevated truck was seated high enough that he could see the glow of the phone screen in my right hand as my left hand held the wheel. I'd had the phone on my thigh, but chose to hold it so I didn't have to keep looking down, taking my eyes off the road. For whatever reason, this infuriated him enough to cause a visceral, over-the-top response. Instantly, feelings of rage washed over me like a violent tsunami—so much that it literally took my breath away. I was drowning in my own anger. For the next few minutes, I wanted to chase down the truck to show him I was just using the GPS; I felt he'd judged me wrongly. Yet a part of me, the side that most men don't want to admit they struggle with, wanted not just to chase him down to justify my use of the phone but to let him see my anger and to "let the games begin." I knew I wouldn't actually resort to violence, but for the next ten minutes my mind played out what I "coulda, shoulda, woulda" done if given the chance to meet up with him. The testosterone and adrenaline pumped through my veins like water being forced through the nozzle of a pressure washer, and I couldn't find the off switch. Two of the man-killers (the lion of disrespect and the Cape buffalo of anger) were coming after me.

Most of us have heard the phrase "fight or flight." The *fight-or-flight response* refers to a specific biochemical reaction that both humans and animals experience during intense stress or fear. The sympathetic nervous system releases hormones that cause changes to occur throughout the body. When a man gets angry, cortisol (a stress hormone) is released; his heart rate, arterial tension, and testosterone production increase, and the left hemisphere of his brain becomes more stimulated. This wash of chemicals is what created the giant wave of anger I experienced. If I had not chosen to renew my mind in the moments that followed, my anger could have driven me to chase down the truck, call out the young man, and give him a piece of my mind.

Cognitive therapy teaches that thoughts create emotions, and those emotions are what will drive our actions. The more intense the emotion, the more extreme the action can become. The theory is that if I can just white-knuckle it and change my actions in that moment, my anger will decrease and I'll soon be sweetly singing, "It is well with my soul." That's called behavior modification. I have never met a person for whom behavior modification made changes in their life that lasted more than a few months. There is a time and a place when behavior modification can be helpful, and the use of antianxiety or depression exercises can certainly help, but unless your core belief system changes, the source of what's making you angry will remain, and all will not be well with your soul.

What causes a man to get angry? We've already discussed the fact that there is righteous anger that is healthy, usually having to do with protecting others. But it is unrighteous, unhealthy anger that causes a man to lash out at others when he feels disrespected or misunderstood. It's what causes young men to fight and grown men to yell (or worse) at their wife and kids. Anger can be like a sword. Healthy anger can cause a man to rise and lift his sword in the right direction, but unhealthy anger can drive him to turn the sword in the wrong direction, devastating those he is meant to defend.

So then, how is a man's behavior not only modified but changed at the core level?

## Changing the Way We Think

> Do not conform to the pattern of this world, but be transformed by the renewing of your mind. Then you will be able to test and approve what God's will is—His good, pleasing and perfect will. (Rom. 12:2)

I want to use three illustrations to help us understand what it is that causes lasting transformation, not just a temporary fix. We'll use the cognitive therapy model to show how our thoughts shape our emotions, and how those emotions shape our actions.

**T-E-A**

If my thought is, *I must succeed*, that thought could create the emotion of anxiety. When the feeling of anxiety takes over, the action arising from that feeling might be that I become a workaholic. If my thought is, *I must succeed in work to be good enough*, I will do everything in my power to achieve that, which will create an unhealthy work ethic. And if that doesn't fix the problem, I will act out to make myself feel better by turning to a temporary fix such as abusing alcohol or drugs to bury the pain, or to something like porn to make me feel excited instead of worthless or depressed. (Actually, studies prove that the opposite happens: when people use porn, they end up feeling *more* worthless and depressed.[1]) We do this when we struggle with needing to perform well and/or needing the good opinions of others to have a sense of self-worth.

## B-T-E-A

Many people think religion is the fix, but applying religion that is based on works—on our own effort—is actually no different from how an unbeliever might deal with the situation. That's because a belief system coming from a theology of *I must do good in order to* be *good* will still leave us with the thought *I must succeed*, leading to anxiety and leaving us with the same actions.

The power of the Good News is that our true identity comes from Christ in us, not from our own effort. It's His effort, and His opinion is the only one that truly matters.

Anyone who suggests that the way to God = Jesus + your own efforts at holiness doesn't understand the true gospel and is spouting heresy—false teaching. Believing this is committing adultery against the Lover of your soul. Unless my beliefs change to "It is Christ in me and *His* performance that give

## Righteousness Applied

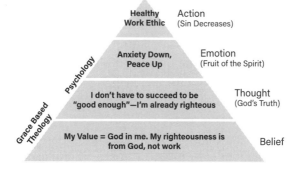

Healthy Work Ethic — Action (Sin Decreases)

Anxiety Down, Peace Up — Emotion (Fruit of the Spirit)

I don't have to succeed to be "good enough"—I'm already righteous — Thought (God's Truth)

My Value = God in me. My righteousness is from God, not work — Belief

Psychology

Grace Based Theology

me my true worth and value," the way I think will remain un-healthy; I'll stay imprisoned in the dysfunctional, performance-based jail cell that created the lies on which I've based my belief system. It's the definition of insanity we've all heard: doing the same thing over and over and expecting different results.

As you can see in this last model, my belief that "My worth and value come from God's righteousness in me" is what changes my unhealthy thoughts. I am being transformed by the renew-ing of my mind as my beliefs line up with God's never-changing truth.

> This righteousness is given through faith in Jesus Christ to all who believe . . . for all have sinned and fall short of the glory of God, and all are justified freely by his grace through the redemption that came by Christ Jesus. (Rom. 3:22–24)

I no longer *have* to succeed to be good enough through my own efforts or others' opinions. Christ is in me! Only under-standing where my true worth and value come from has the transforming power to reshape my thoughts, emotions, and actions. When my thoughts line up with truth, my emotions become healthy, leading me to healthy actions. The challenges we face are actually gifts; they help us practice bringing our thoughts—and consequently, our emotions and actions—into alignment with the truth.

Modern thinking and motivational speakers will try to con-vince us that in order to have a positive view of ourselves, we must learn to accept ourselves, love ourselves, and develop self-esteem. That's their solution to a wonderful life. But trying to persuade ourselves that we are good enough just the way we are creates anxiety, frustration, and hopelessness because *we are not good enough just the way we are without Christ!* It's nearly impossible for us to "like" ourselves when we repeatedly think, feel, and act so badly. When that's our core belief, we will naturally turn to our own performance and other people's opinions as a barometer to measure if we're good enough.

◀◀◀◁▷▶▶

What does all this have to do with the heated exchange between me and the raging man in the truck? What was it that finally calmed the unhealthy emotions tempting me to chase him down on a busy highway? **Renewing my mind.**

In the minutes following his angry response, I experienced a plethora of unhealthy emotions. I can identify emotions by using the words "I feel" before them. A guy watching his football team play might say, "I feel like they're going to lose," but what he really means is "I *think* (or believe) they're going to lose," because he's really describing his thoughts or beliefs about whether or not his team will win, not his feelings. If I am talking about feelings—emotions—I say, "I feel angry, I feel jealous, I feel hopeless, lustful, depressed," and so on.

How did I know my emotions were unhealthy? Because unhealthy emotions line up with the deeds of the flesh as found in

Galatians 5:19–21, such as sexual immorality, impurity, hatred, and jealousy.

When I'm believing what is true, my thoughts create emotions that line up with the fruit of the Spirit in Galatians 5:22–23. I feel loving, joyful, peaceful, patient, kind, good, faithful, gentle, and self-controlled. Because I wasn't experiencing the fruit of the Spirit, I knew that there were lies twisted in with what I was thinking. That's why my fight-or-flight reactions were triggered: I was buying into lies, and those lies had to be replaced with truth. If we don't first replace the lies with truth, and then renew our minds with that truth, nothing will change.

As I wrestled with my anger (and I mean *really* wrestled with it), because I knew the truth of what I just wrote, I was eventually able to land in a good place before any lasting damage could be done. Here's what my thought process looked like as I renewed my mind:

1. *I reminded myself of my true identity: "Christ in me."*
   The guy in the truck had nothing to do with my righteousness. That comes from God. This man didn't create me, I didn't answer to him, and I didn't need his good opinion of me to understand that I'm already good enough in God's eyes.

2. *I asked questions and used empathy.* I attempted to "walk in his shoes." What was it that made him so angry to elicit such an intense response? And why did I

feel the need to blame him and defend myself? Trying to understand someone else's actions or reactions can only be done when we don't have to win a disagreement. As soon as I feel like I *have* to win, I've already lost because I will resort to blaming and defending. Only by trying to understand the other person can I truly care about them. When I blame and defend, I'm going into self-protection mode, which is all about my needs.

Empathizing with a person who has really angered us isn't an easy thing to do. We want to bite back—to get even. It's only when we can take personal responsibility and lead with humility that the conflict can begin to be disarmed. This is what takes the venom out of the enemy's bite and stops the man-killers in their tracks.

## Quieting My Angry Roar

As I began trying to understand where this man might have been coming from with his seemingly misdirected anger, the Holy Spirit reminded me of my own anger and bitterness toward someone who'd changed my life and my family's life forever through the use of a cell phone while driving. In January 2013, while stopped at a traffic light, my parents were hit from behind by a young driver who was on her phone. My mother broke her leg, and my father had severe brain damage that left him in a coma for several months and then unable to walk for the rest of his life. The stress and physical strain of taking care of my father took an enormous toll on my mother's health. They had to sell both their winter home in Florida and their home in Pennsylvania to be able to afford to move into a dark, cramped handicap-accessible apartment. I watched my mother's knees buckle as she saw their life's belongings sold at a garage sale. Things they'd saved for and chosen together—their dreams—were now being picked over by nameless people grabbing things for pennies on the dollar. It was agony hearing my father cry out for his siblings, most of whom had passed years earlier, as his mind wasn't working correctly. My mother had to call 911 over and over because Dad kept falling out of his home hospital bed during the night; he'd wake up thinking he could still walk, or dream there was a fire and would manipulate himself over the side rail to try to get to his beloved wife as she slept. His adult diaper would need to be changed several times a day and cream applied to skin that was sore and irritated from being bedridden.

My memories of what happened to them and to the rest of our family, solely because of someone's choice to use a cell phone while driving, welled up in my mind. The rage I felt minutes before was now replaced with understanding, compassion, sympathy, repentance, tears, and personal responsibility. I no longer wanted to run the truck down and fight the angry passenger. I wanted to let him know that he was right, that I shouldn't have been on my phone, and that I was sorry for my poor choice and would make appropriate changes so I wouldn't endanger myself or others by using my cell phone while driving. This wasn't about whether his choice of words, demeanor, or actions were appropriate; it was about me moving from an unhealthy place into a healthy one. It wasn't about his anger—I couldn't control that. It was about me dealing with my own anger. There was truth in what he was saying to me, and when I was willing to acknowledge that truth, it defused my anger.

Many of us have learned to use an angry roar when we feel disrespected or misunderstood. It's how we attempt to gain control when we feel out of control. That roar is not coming from our core but from our flesh, which is always coveting, always striving to get what we want, forgetting we already have everything we'll ever need. It's *that* roar that needs to be quieted. However, there is a time and a place to listen to the roar within—when it comes from a *righteous* anger, a roar that is not rooted in our flesh but deep within the character of God. It can lead us to protect the vulnerable, stop the abuser, care for the widow, father the fatherless, and engage in battle against the enemy's lies that keep attacking God's beloved.

## THE **BIG** QUESTION:

Challenges are gifts. Sometimes the most difficult things we go through become the very things we need to find healing for ourselves and to extend forgiveness to others. When we choose not to forgive or not to even attempt to understand the choice of someone who has sinned against us, we stay angry, causing us to remain in a prison of our own choosing. Is there someone whom you're struggling to forgive? Try to understand them by thinking of the situation from their point of view. Does trying to understand what they might have gone through soften your heart and affect your ability to extend empathy? Is forgiveness our gift to God, or God's gift to us?

# The Big Five Man-Killers #4

## LUST

### (Elephant)

**E**lephants are not always easy to see. I've been close enough to an elephant to hit it with a rock and still didn't see it standing right in front of a tree. That sounds crazy, but it's true. However, once you know what to look for, you can't miss it.

An elephant will uproot a large tree to get at its leaves, bark, and branches, not realizing it causes the tree to die and never bear fruit again. It takes what it wants and leaves a trail of destruction in its wake. Lust is a man-killer that will knock a man's beliefs, values, and convictions off track and keep him pursuing things that can destroy not only his family and career but also his mind and soul. When a man covets that big promotion, he will do whatever it takes to achieve that title. When he lusts after a woman, he will do whatever it takes to win her attention. When he believes he's not getting what he deserves sexually at home, he may turn to porn and/or affairs. Why? Because he thinks having a better title, having a beautiful woman, or fantasizing about a woman willingly performing whatever he desires without rejecting him will affirmatively answer his question, "Do I have what it takes?" The dangerous thing is when those things seem to work for him. They actually only work temporarily, because they leave God out and create a false identity. "There is a way that seems right to a man, but its end is the way to death" (Prov. 14:12 NKJV). They might satisfy his desires for a moment, but lust in any form always leads to wanting more, and the man will be tyrannized. He will continue wanting more and more of what he thinks he "has to have" and will uproot everything he has worked for and believed in to satisfy his lustful desires.

Men are visually stimulated. It was no accident that God made a woman with beautiful curves. Curves are attractive even with sports cars. Those sleek lines on a Porsche or Corvette weren't put there purely for aerodynamics; they grab our attention. It's those curves that make some of the most alluring cars in the world so attractive, even if they don't do zero to sixty in three seconds flat. Curves can also be seductive, and it's the curves on a woman's body that play on a man's thoughts and, if he isn't in a good place mentally, can draw him into taking more than a glance. He doesn't just want to pluck the apple from the tree—he wants to *taste* it. Before he knows it, he's not just taken a second glance; he's now playing out in his mind what it would be like not just to *see* her body but to *have* her. He wants to consume the apple.

When addressing a group of over three hundred men at a recent retreat, I brought up this topic. When I asked the question, "How many of you struggle when you see a good-looking woman wearing yoga pants?" nearly every man in that room raised his hand, except for a few who were raising their toes inside their shoes. Who in that room was more at risk—the men who quickly raised their hands, admitting their struggle, or the ones who didn't because they were worried that their fig leaf wasn't hiding enough?

Lust is a man-killer; it can drive a man into hiding through shame as he feels like he *should* be able to control his lustful desires on his own. Many men leave God out of their struggle for a couple of reasons. One reason is that he is getting something out of his struggle (sin feels good). The other is because he feels like he isn't good enough if he can't conquer his unhealthy emotions on his own. He has been taught that if he can't escape the power of lust through sin management (try harder), he must not be good enough. Both of those reasons are why lust is so deadly and a man-killer. They both leave their victims ashamed.

## Is She on the Menu?

I was having dinner with a friend who was really struggling with looking at women. When the server came to take our order, we couldn't help noticing that she was extremely attractive. After pouring our coffee, she realized we didn't have menus, apologized, and left to go grab some. As she walked away, he leaned out, stared at her figure, and commented, "I wonder if she's on the menu." That sounds offensive—it absolutely *is* offensive—but he was verbalizing what many insecure men think. Many men view a woman's body as a piece of raw meat and will do whatever it takes to have her at least mentally and sometimes physically. Some men outwardly flirt and stare at a woman to see if they can get her to play along in an attempt to make themselves feel wanted. Inwardly, their question is, *Would a woman like that be interested in a man like me?* Unfortunately, the truth in either case is that this man is struggling with his identity, even if he's looking at a woman as an object just to get the chemical rush in his brain from lusting.

When a predator has enough food in front of him to sustain him, he's focused on what he has and has no need to seek additional prey. Likewise, when a man discovers that all his needs are already met in Christ, he doesn't need to objectify women to get that dopamine rush. Being secure in your one, true identity is a powerful, transformative thing.

Not too long after that, this friend called me on the phone. He'd decided to meet with one of his church elders, who was almost ninety years old. After he explained to the elder that he struggled with looking at beautiful women, the elder replied, "So, what are *we* going to do about that?" No matter what age a man is, until his question is answered about where his true identity comes from, he will struggle with lust.

I received a private message late one night from a woman I'll call Tammy, who had been in town for a friend's wedding. She'd recently gotten divorced and had remarried a few months afterward. She and her new husband planned to fly home the following evening, but she'd spent the night separated from her husband at a friend's house because they'd had a huge fight the night of her friend's wedding. She was struggling with anxiety and having severe panic attacks, and she asked if I could meet with her in a public location the next morning. After she'd informed her husband that she'd reached out to me and he agreed to our meeting, I accepted.

Before our server could even set the glasses of water on our table, she began railing to me about her husband. "I can't believe this! I got divorced because my ex-husband never paid attention to me, and now my new husband can't keep his eyes off other women! He gets his jollies from gawking at other women—not from me. I am so done with men—they're just pigs!" She told me that everything seemed great in her new marriage—until she started noticing he was constantly looking at other women. After a few drinks at the wedding reception, he'd begun to stare at almost every woman, including her best friend, who was the maid of honor. He was not just looking at the women but staring them up and down.

As I waited for her to come up for air, I took out my notebook and wrote down a few notes. Whenever I meet with someone, I typically write down the emotions I hear as they dump. I know those emotions are coming from whatever the person is thinking, and their thoughts stem from what they believe to be true. What I heard from Tammy included anger, fear, rage, doubt, worry, insecurity, loneliness, and betrayal.

After Tammy slowed her words, I finally spoke up. "First, I want you to know how sorry I am for you that you've had to endure so much rejection in your life. That must be terribly hard," I said. "And I want you to know that I'm also sorry that your husband has been buying into the lies of the enemy that he needs to look at women to make himself feel better. It's obvious he's addicted to the chemical wash his brain gets from lusting." I no sooner got that last sentence out of my mouth when she again opened up her pressure release valve, but this time her tone ratcheted up ten times and revealed the real source of her hurt and fears. "You're sorry that he's bought into lies causing him to look at other women? What about *me*? I'm the one who's not good enough here. If I was good enough, he'd only be looking at me! And honestly, I'm starting to enjoy it when other men stare at me. At least it makes me feel like there's someone out there who wants me."

Silence.

Tammy sat there, her words lingering in the air like a heavy fog. She was adamant that she wasn't struggling with jealousy, that she was secure in her own identity. She kept insisting that this was "his problem." And she was absolutely correct that he had a problem—but so did she. She was getting her worth and value from whether her husband gave her the attention and happiness she believed she deserved. That had been the story with her previous husband, and now she wanted other men to pay attention to her so she could feel better about herself. She was lusting after their lust!

When I asked her what she did whenever she saw her husband looking at women, she said she let him see how angry she was by degrading and emasculating him in front of others. She admitted she hoped that embarrassing him would change his behavior. Then I asked her how that was working for her. Tammy responded, "It doesn't. It just makes things worse, and then I'm the one left feeling embarrassed and insecure."

I finally asked her, "Tammy, what would happen if you didn't connect your worth and value to your husband? What if you didn't need him or other men looking at you in order to feel good enough?" Clearly not filtering her response, she blurted out, "I'd for sure be a lot happier and maybe actually love myself for the first time!" Hearing that, I immediately asked, "So, what I hear you saying is that you'd be a lot happier if you weren't so codependent, right?" She sat there looking dazed. "Tammy, what if at your core you truly believed you were already good enough, that your worth and value didn't have to come from men? What if your good enough came from the righteousness of Christ that is in you and not from whether you felt your husband was physically attracted to you? If you truly believed that, would you need to throw a fit and try to make him feel worse about himself? What might be different?"

Tammy slowly began nodding her head up and down, and then she laughed. "I might just go stand in front of him when he's looking at another woman and say, 'Baby, why would you want to be looking at hamburger when you could have prime rib?'" "Exactly!" I said. "Confidence is extremely attractive. Tammy, in essence, you're wanting your husband to fill your needs in a similar way to how he looks at other women to meet his own needs. Whenever we attempt to get our good enough from anything or anyone other than God, it's idolatry. In that moment we are lusting for more worth and value, and thus committing adultery against Jesus Christ."

Tammy's face began to change. I could see she knew her own unhealthiness had been exposed, but somehow it was okay because it helped her release her anger and judgment against her husband. "Who is the only one you can fix?" I asked. "Myself," she responded. "Tammy, whenever we attempt to keep another person's side of the street clean, our side starts looking like a garbage dump. Our job is to keep *our* side of the street clean. The other person may never change their behavior, but you are not responsible for that. There's a good chance that as you become healthier, your lust for attention will decrease; his may as well, but there are no guarantees. The good news is you will be okay because you will no longer need to carry his unhealthiness on your back. And no matter what happens, you're going to be okay because your identity is in Christ."

The elephant in the room had just been destroyed. Identity in Christ is a lust-killer!

## THE **BIG** QUESTION:

When a man doesn't feel like he's enough, he can take his question to a woman, even if she's only an image on a screen. What is it about porn or having an affair that can be so attractive to a man? Does he ever get his question of "Am I good enough?" truly answered by taking it anywhere other than to God?

# Naked and Afraid

Then the Lᴏʀᴅ God called to the man, and said to him, "Where are you?" He said, "I heard the sound of You in the garden, and I was afraid because I was naked; so I hid myself." And He said, "Who told you that you were naked?"

GENESIS 3:9–11 NASB

ountains. Forests. Lakes. Rushing streams. Sunrise. Sunset. Wild animals. Night skies filled with an endless number of brilliant stars, planets, and shooting stars. Majesty. The earthy smell of the forest floor that crackles underfoot. The flick of an ear and twitch of a tail of a deer totally in tune with its surroundings. The sound of the wind as it whispers through the pines all around me, beckoning me to follow. I feel as if I'm being watched and summoned by a power much greater than my eyes can see, greater than I can comprehend or dream up—and I am. This is creation, and its Maker is everywhere. Infinite. Perfect. Never sleeping. Always at work. Always calling.

I carefully unzip my sleeping bag as quietly as I can so as not to wake the men sleeping on both sides of me. The embers of the campfire are now just a dim glow as the predawn dew settles. As I rise, I feel the cold of the night slip into my warm cocoon and my senses adjust to my surroundings; I'm staring, listening, searching the darkness. The one thing I know is that I'm here, in this place, waiting for something to quicken me, to start my purpose for this new day. It's like the wind in the pines is speaking to me, inviting me to move. It's always been like this, for as long as I can remember. Always.

As the heaviness of sleep begins to lift, I remember where I am: I'm leading a men's retreat deep in the mountains of Idaho. As I quietly get dressed, I can hear the scattered unzipping of sleeping bags and clicking of flashlights as each man comes to life. Something is inside us, awakening us, pulling us toward something we are longing for. We think it's a destination, a place where we can finally be content—happy—at peace. What we are longing for does exist; we just have to discover that it's not seen by our physical eyes but is something deep within our cores that can only be seen through the eyes of the eternal part of us—our spirits. This weekend men will learn to see in a new way, from the inside out.

The men roll up their sleeping bags and begin moving through the darkness down the winding gravel path to the lake. More lights gleam through the trees as we come together this morning for one purpose: to spend time with our Creator.

Mist fills the air, and the predawn light illuminates a magical mist rising from the surface of the lake. Mysterious and wonderful, it is something that only those who show up this early in the day are privileged to behold. The gray wooden docks are still, and nearby on the shore, the camp canoes are lined up in a row, waiting for the next adventurer to flip one over and paddle off to discover new places. A loon sounds off, alerting all that the glory of God is once again being revealed to those who have eyes to see.

Through the fog we hear a small motorboat in the distance as an elderly fisherman navigates his craft to a spot he's fished for decades. The tips of his poles, already prepared with lures, dangle off the bow and point the way to where he'll anchor. He knows his way there. He doesn't need a map or a GPS; full of wonder and adventure, the seasoned fisherman knows when it's time to shut off the motor, drop anchor, and make that first cast into the virgin stillness of a new day. He has a hope for what he'll encounter—and so do the men lined up along the lakeshore.

These men have journeyed for hours to be here. "Here" is not just the location; "here" is a place where they can get away from the rush and struggles of their predictable, monotonous lives. They have made this journey longing to have an awakening of what they think are their souls, but what they're longing for is an awakening of their spirits. They don't know yet that there is a huge difference between the soul and the spirit: one is temporary and flesh, the other is eternal and contains all the power that created everything there is.

After our time on the lake asking God to reveal to us what He wants us to see, the men head back for coffee, eggs, and bacon. There's nothing like the smell of coffee and bacon in the morning to get a man's stomach and his brain to engage in unison. When the last plate has been scraped and coffees topped off, the men gather their Bibles and notebooks and make their way to the chairs arranged in the front of the room. They're awake now, and talking sports, work, politics, money. The fellowship they were seeking with God they are now seeking with each other. There's only one problem: most of them are trying to fit in. It's like a masquerade ball where each man is trying to find his "good enough."

Throughout the retreat, one man after another comes to share their stories with me. These men, who seem tough and like they have it all together in public, now come up to me privately to reveal they are emotionally threadbare, desperate, and guilt-ridden. As tears fill their eyes, they share their struggles with pornography, alcohol, affairs, job loss, divorce, broken families, and hopelessness.

At one point I spoke to the group about Africa's Big Five. I love using the wilds of nature to grab a man's attention, then relate it back to the home front. As I typically do, I then redirected the conversation from Africa's Big Five to the big five needs of men and women. As I also did in my book *Into the*

*Wilds*, I recounted a staff meeting at church when the marriage book *His Needs, Her Needs* came up. It was not pretty, and it left the men in that meeting wanting to crawl under the table. Here's how the conversation went.

My friend Derek wrote the top five needs of a woman according to *His Needs, Her Needs* on the board. As he wrote, I watched the men and women in the room. Some of the women crossed their arms and a couple smiled, while the men shook their heads, sighed, or just waited for the boot to drop.

Women's "big five" needs:

1. Affection
2. Conversation
3. Honesty
4. Financial support
5. Family commitment

After writing the big five on the board, Derek asked all the men in the room to rate the importance of each of the women's needs on a scale of 1–10, with 10 being the most important. Here were the results—how these men scored what women viewed as their top five needs:

1. Affection: 10
2. Conversation: 10
3. Honesty: 10

4. Financial support: 10
5. Family commitment: 10

There were no smart-aleck responses from the men; there was more of a sense of shame knowing that they had not done their best in each area. The women's responses affirmed how important each need was to them and how it made them feel secure and loved when their man met each of these needs.

Next, Derek wrote down the top five needs of a man from the book.

Men's "big five" needs:

1. Sexual fulfillment
2. Recreational companionship
3. An attractive spouse
4. Domestic support
5. Admiration

Before Derek even wrote down the second item, all the women in the room began to mock and complain. (These responses were those of the women in our staff meeting; they may not reflect how all or even most women feel.)

1. Sexual fulfillment
   The women exclaimed, "That's all men want—*sex*! That's all they think about! Men just need to find a

bathroom to get their frustrations out and quit expecting women to do their dirty work for them!" The look on the men's faces was unanimous: *Whoa! Where did that come from?!*

2. Recreational companionship
   "That's all men want is a woman to go and do whatever *he* wants to do!"

3. An attractive spouse
   "We can't compete with the young things you're looking at on porn sites and TV commercials. If that's what you want, you can just go find yourself some eighteen-year-old to fulfill your fantasies with—we're outta here!"

4. Domestic support
   "All men want is a woman to pick up after them. You can clean the dang house yourself!" (finger snap included)

5. Admiration
   "You just want women to worship the ground you walk on while we get nothing in return."

Here's how the women scored what the men viewed as their top five needs:

1. Sexual Fulfillment: 2
2. Recreational Companionship: 2

3. An Attractive Spouse: 1
4. Domestic Support: 2
5. Admiration: -10

Taken aback, one of the men then spoke up: "Ladies, now you can see why men feel so disrespected. According to your words, body language, and how you scored men's needs, you believe men's needs aren't important!" The remaining men nodded in agreement. The underbelly of men's anger had just been exposed.

Derek then used this illustration to open up more conversation: "Imagine a wife saying, 'If only my husband would talk to me more, it would make life so much easier,' and the husband responds, 'I have no interest in being feminized, so I'm not going to talk the rest of the way home.' How would it feel to the wife to have her need for communication kicked to the curb like that? Or how would the woman have reacted if her husband would have said to her, 'I'll listen to you, but you need to take your clothes off first'? She would have been deeply hurt, and rightfully so—left feeling cheap and degraded, used for only her body."

The room fell silent.

Now, you might be feeling validated right now if you're a man—maybe even angry. And women might feel like men's needs are mostly made up, or these needs have been used to excuse abuse for so long and so widely they are no longer valid, but there is biblical support for men's needs as well as for women's. Men's and women's needs are different, but the needs of both are equally important. It's easy to see why men disappear to the garage or the wilderness; those are the places where they can sort through the external condemning voices of society and get in touch with their inner man, a place where they can find their "good enough."

It's evident from that illustration why men have these buried feelings of being dirty or not being good enough; modern society places a much higher value on a woman's needs than a man's. Now, there's no doubt that a man's needs can be twisted into something unhealthy if he's believing and acting on lies, but so can a woman's.

When a man feels that his wife doesn't care about meeting his needs, he's an open target for the enemy to flip healthy needs into lust as he feels like she's not only kicking him to the curb but also kicking him right between the legs . . . with size 13 steel-toed boots!

I was speaking with a man who shared with me that he would text his wife throughout the day, as life had gotten very busy for both of them and that was their primary daytime communication. Every time he would text his wife something about how he couldn't wait to have "alone time" with her, she would text back "SMH" (shaking my head) usually followed by, "Is that all you ever think about?" After getting enough of those responses, the man said, "I quit talking about sexual intimacy altogether because I felt dirty. I even began dying to sex because I thought I must not be enough for her or she wouldn't be mocking my physical needs." Over time, the man said, rather than going to her to meet his physical needs, it was much easier to just go to porn because the woman on the screen wouldn't say "SMH" and sexually reject him.

Obviously, porn isn't right, isn't healthy, and isn't what God intended. God designed a healthy marriage relationship to include sexual intimacy, but He designed it to include emotional and spiritual intimacy as well. A woman isn't like a microwave; she's more like a slow cooker. She isn't moved to physical intimacy through you flexing your bicep, dragging her out of the house to show her the buck in the back of your truck, or hearing you incessantly talk about your achievements. She wants to know that you want to know *her*. She needs to hear you ask, "Do you know what I love about you?" She longs to hear you blurt out, "You look amazing!" Sometimes she needs to hear you swallow your pride and just say the words, "You're right." Even saying the classic "I love you" can get you out of the batter's box and to first base. I heard a man say one time, "Honey, I told you I loved you thirty years ago. If anything changes, you'll be the first to know." Guys, that's a definite strikeout. Just remember that moving her heart isn't like setting the microwave for a minute. Would you rather have a flavorless heated-up burrito from a convenience store or a slow-cooked pot roast that falls apart with the slightest touch?

I just ran that last paragraph past my wife to hear her response. Her body language totally changed as I read it, and she said, "That is *exactly* right." Home run. When it comes down to brass tacks, intimacy is actually what both men *and* women are longing for—it just looks different for each of us.

One thing you'll discover if you work with men is that they don't like to talk about their emotions. They would rather tough it out—suck it up, hike up their big boy panties, and fake it till they make it—than talk about how they really feel deep inside, because somehow that makes them feel weak. Nothing could be further from the truth! But that's what society has taught men *and* women. It's sad to say, but many women have bought into the lie that men *should* just tough it out rather than become vulnerable, because that's what society says is strong.

The truth is, **being vulnerable takes more strength than hiding**. But it's only possible when one feels safe. For many women, something that makes them feel safe is for their husbands to talk with and listen to them. For many men, part of what makes them feel safe with their wives, and therefore *able* to talk with and listen to them, is physical touch and closeness. To ask a man to communicate and reveal his innermost thoughts and feelings without physical closeness is like a man asking a woman to take all her clothes off without any romance or foreplay. It leaves both of them feeling manipulated and used.

The beautiful thing is that when a man does move toward his wife with affection and communication, she will usually respond to meet his needs as well. But men are becoming more and more emasculated in today's society and have lost their roar, their true voice that is a reflection of the Lion of Judah. It's a voice that moves young men and boys to want to be that man who commands respect and attention; a voice that resonates from deep within; a voice that is given to him when he finally realizes his true identity. And the enemy is doing everything he can to silence that voice. Why? Because when a man knows who he really is, he's beautifully dangerous to the core.

*Who is* that authentic man, and what has caused him to stay indoors where life is safe and predictable—and boring? What or who has caused him to lose his sense of wonderment and adventure? Who lied to man, telling him that unless he performs in such a way that he's accepted by others, he's not good enough? Who silenced his roar? Who told him he should feel naked without the approval of others?

## Naked and Afraid

One of my earliest memories was being seen partially naked by my sister at about the age of five. I'd left the bathroom door partway open, and she walked in while I was pulling my pants up. Her quick reaction was to cover her eyes and slam the door, which left me feeling like something was wrong. I ran to my mother screaming, "She saw me naked!" As I ran to tattle, my sister was behind me, yelling, "He left the door open!" I'm sure my mother would have responded differently if she'd had a few moments to think, but instead she scolded my sister and sent her to her room. In that moment, shame for both of us crept in. My sister was getting punished for accidentally walking in on me, while I was being coddled as if my nakedness was bad and I was a victim.

Many of us would have handled that situation in a similar fashion, but what if we were able to respond without shame, fear, or giving punishment in a knee-jerk reaction? What if we could shed the shame attached to our nakedness like a snake sheds its skin? The reason snakes shed is to allow for continued growth and to remove parasites that may have attached to their old skin. Shame is like a parasite that sticks with us, keeping us from being able to experience the life God planned for us.

From the beginning in the Garden of Eden, Satan has been the great liar. That slimy belly-crawler who lusted to be like God poisoned Adam and Eve with his lies, bringing shame and fear into a world of unspeakable beauty and peace.

In the second and third chapters of Genesis, we can see that God's command to Adam was very clear: "You must not eat from the tree of the knowledge of good and evil" (Gen. 2:17). It didn't take long for the serpent to poison Eve with doubt: "Did God *really* say . . . ?" After Eve reminded the serpent, "God has said, 'You shall not eat from it or touch it, or you will die,'" Satan sank his fangs in all the way: "You won't really die; God just doesn't want you to be like Him!"

When God called out asking Adam, "Where are you?" Adam replied, "I heard the sound of You in the garden, and

I was afraid because I was naked, so I hid myself." God's next question is key: "*Who told you* that you were naked?" BUSTED.

Up until that point, Adam and Eve had walked through the garden feeling no shame or fear. They enjoyed the mountains and streams, felt the breeze awaken their senses, walked without fear or condemnation. But in one vicious strike, the lies of the evil one left them both hiding in shame, knowing they were naked, and afraid of their Father, their Creator. My circumstance left me behind my locked bedroom door, afraid and ashamed. But *why*? What about my nakedness made me feel ashamed or dirty? Where did that lie come from? How many men have grown up feeling inadequate and have given in to lust, falling into porn addictions or affairs seeking validation? I found myself blaming my sister for my mistake of leaving the bathroom door open; I was convinced I was a victim. Sin's venom had already penetrated my young mind, leaving me feeling naked and afraid.

These kinds of attacks are exactly what the enemy planned to destroy God's glorious creation. His poisonous plot is to keep us from seeing ourselves in God's perfect image, trying to get our "good enough" through our works, through our performance, through the eyes of how others see us—that we should be identified by the labels of our sins and carry their shame. The enemy's lies are what cause us to forget that our one true voice came from the Creator who spoke us into existence. The reason your heavenly Father created you was not because of what good you could do for Him, but because He desired you. Period.

Satan's lie: you are naked, guilty, and condemned. You're not good enough.

God's truth: at your core, your spirit, you are clothed in His righteousness because you've been forgiven, redeemed, and filled with His promised Holy Spirit, making you 100 percent complete *in Him*. This is not because of your good works or performance but because of what Jesus did for you through His death and resurrection. Because of Jesus, you are good enough!

## THE **BIG** QUESTION:

Where have you felt invalidated in your "top five" needs? Has something ever happened to you that caused you to feel naked and afraid?

# The Big Five Man-Killers #5

## SHAME

*(Leopard)*

If you've caught a glimpse of one of Africa's big cats, especially a leopard, you are one of the lucky few. I've driven hundreds of miles across the African plains filming the Big Five, and leopards are the real ghosts of the darkness. They are feared hunters with the muscles of a bodybuilder and can run twice as fast as a human. If leopards had the heart of a lion, they would rule the plains. Their stealth, acute hearing (five times better than humans), and ability to hunt in the dark of night make leopards virtually undetectable. Although full-grown male leopards weigh in at only about 165 pounds, their nearly three-inch canines; retractable claws; and ability to run at up to forty miles per hour, jump forward twenty feet and into the air ten feet, and kill an animal with one swift bite to the neck make them one of the world's most-feared and deadliest killers.

The thing about cats, whether domestic or wild, is that they are ruthless killing machines. They're master stalkers, and they don't just hunt to eat; sometimes they kill just for the thrill of the hunt. Cats are the ultimate predator, and they do most of their hunting in the dark.

One of South Africa's most well-known big-game guides, Dries Visser Sr., was attacked by a wounded leopard after one of his hunters made a poor shot while hunting with Dries Visser Safaris. While Dries was searching for the leopard, it sprang from the long grass, taking him to the ground. A leopard will dig its claws into a victim's scalp with one paw, lock onto a shoulder with the other, then grab its prey by the neck and sink its long canines into the throat. Once it has a good hold, it'll disembowel its catch with the claws of its powerful hind legs (exactly what housecats do when they're in a fight). A leopard can turn out the lights on its victim in a snap. Knowing all this, Dries immediately shoved his fist in the leopard's mouth, keeping it from being able to clamp down on his throat. As fate would have it, the leopard's hind legs weren't working correctly as a result of the misplaced rifle shot. That is what kept Dries alive until those who heard his screams could get to him and dispatch the beast.

Sometime in the minutes that followed, they sat Dries on a picnic table and bandaged up his hand and wrist where the leopard had fileted his skin down to the bone. Several days after the attack, a friend sent me pictures of him sitting there, bandaged and bloody, one ear nearly torn off from the leopard's claws. Dries was *smiling*! I asked my friend, "Why was Dries smiling?" The response: "If you'd just survived a tornado of teeth and claws trying to tear *you* limb from limb, you'd be smiling too!" Thankfully, Dries's father had instructed him many times as a boy that the first thing to do if attacked by a leopard is get your fist in its mouth so it can't get its mouth around your neck. Dries had renewed his mind many times with this lesson, and it saved his life.

In ancient Roman culture, a murderer's punishment was to be forced to have the corpse of his victim strapped to his bare back wherever he went. This was done so that the murderer would not only see and smell the rottenness of his sin but the maggot-infested corpse would also infect the criminal, causing a slow, painful, stench-filled, shameful death. A leopard, after devouring its kill in a tree, leaves what's left of the carcass at the base of the tree once it's done eating. That's how you find leopard trees. It's an eerie feeling when you walk up and see and smell the rotting corpses all around you. The same holds true with how Satan works. He drags up both our deepest sins and those which others have committed against us, then, by his lies, straps them to our backs like corpses, where we can feel their weight and continue to experience the devastation they caused. He doesn't want us to know that we are dead to sin but *alive in Christ*.

Why am I talking about a decaying corpse being strapped onto its killer's back? Because I work with men almost daily who have the dead weight of shame on their backs, and the scary thing is that they've learned to live with it—if you can call that living. They are dead men walking.

Lack of purpose, craving for respect, anger, lust, bitterness, unforgiveness, worthlessness, resentment . . . these all create shame, which can lead to depression, acting out, or even more serious mental disorders if not healed. Shame leaves rotting corpses all around because of something we did or something that was said or done to us in the past, months or even years ago. Over time, shame leaks its poison into its victims, and the weight of it bends us over in excruciating pain.

My wife is a survivor. What Stacy went through growing up no child should ever have to endure. She grew up fatherless, had to sleep on a mattress on the floor in her mother's bedroom surrounded by dog feces and cockroaches, was repeatedly exposed to sexual behavior, was left alone many nights with not much more than a bottle of vodka in the fridge, was abandoned by her mother at the age of eight, and was sexually abused by a babysitter as a young child and by a police officer in her teen years (who wasn't charged, as it was his word against hers and he was a relative of a very famous gospel singer). There is so much more, but I think this grim picture is enough to show why she was tortured by abuse and abandonment issues for most of her life. She came to believe that abuse and abandonment were what she deserved.

I've hunted big game all over the world. I'm on the pro staff of many outdoor companies because I've worked hard to be good at what I do. I'm not afraid to venture into the dark before light to pursue my prey because I carry the right weapon and I know how to use it. I've been charged by some of the largest and most ferocious animals on the planet. But just days before sitting down to write this chapter, I encountered a different animal—one that no amount of wilderness training or earthly weapons could take down. This was something much bigger, and it left me feeling helpless.

I found Stacy in our walk-in closet, curled up in the fetal position. Something had happened to trigger her childhood memories, and just like a little girl, she hid in the closet—the only place she had felt safe as a child. Like a housecat playing with its victim, Satan was preying on Stacy's wounds of abandonment, playing with her mind, creating a gut-wrenching episode of PTSD. The enemy knew he couldn't kill her true identity in Christ, so he tried to steal, kill, and destroy her happiness and peace of mind.

After almost an hour of my talking her down, Stacy came out of the closet only to begin pacing back and forth like a caged animal, venomous words spewing out of her mouth about what had been done to her. I became the thick ice she jumped on, hoping it wouldn't crack. Some of her comments were directed at me, and some were hurtful, but I knew they weren't coming from the *real* Stacy, who is secure in Christ. They were coming from the dark nights and places in her life where she'd been left unprotected.

She paced back and forth for almost forty-five minutes, and then, as quickly as the episode had begun, it ended. Stacy came crashing down, apologizing for her rant. Within seconds, deep-seated shame took over as she began to beat herself up for her actions. If you don't understand someone's story or the depths of complex PTSD, you might try to "fix" the sufferer by saying things like, "It doesn't matter if you have a father; you know your heavenly Father," or "That's in the past—you need to get over it." Or you might throw "scriptural prescriptions" at them, not realizing that this only adds more shame to someone who in that moment truly is not in their right mind. No matter what your intentions, all this does is add another dead corpse to the one they're already carrying, and the weight can become so devastating that they contemplate taking their own life. We need to be willing to stick it out when things get rough and be secure enough in our own identity to simply listen as they deal with the ghosts of their past in the midst of their darkest moments. Loving like that requires us to love like God loves.

> Watch what God does, and then you do it, like children who learn proper behavior from their parents. Mostly what God does is love you. Keep company with him and learn a life of love. Observe how Christ loved us. His love was not cautious but extravagant. He didn't love in order to get something from us but to give everything of himself to us. Love like that. (Eph. 5:1–2 MSG)

Satan is a thief who wants to rob you of your worth and value and rip out any sense of purpose that remains in you. Jesus said, "The thief has come to steal, kill, and destroy." Similarly, that's what big cats do—just for the pleasure of it—and they do it in the darkness. How does the enemy accomplish this task? He drives you into the dark places, then controls you using his best weapon: *shame*. Satan guilts people into believing that performance-based striving will create soul transformation. Shame will rot your soul (your mind, will, thoughts, and emotions). After Jesus says that the thief has come to steal, kill, and destroy, He goes on to say, "I have come that they may have life, and have it to the full" (John 10:10).

What is the greatest way to tell if you're buying into the lies of the thief or walking in the truth of Christ? The thief whispers lies of fear and shame, the language of the dead and dying, to bleed you out and drive you into the darkness. Jesus beckons you into the light with promises of hope and love, proclaiming His victory over death through the power of His crucifixion and resurrection.

While writing this segment, I reached out to a group of men through social media and asked them where in their lives they found themselves being most afraid. I thought I'd get some really honest, right-off-the-bone responses, but mostly what came back were the nice, safe, religious answers I was trying to get away from. Men weren't sharing what was really going on under the hood; they were too worried about how they'd look and about their answers getting out somehow,

deepening their shame. The enemy uses shame to make a believer think he has to *look* good in order to *be* good. Once the
believer buys into that lie, it's like a snake trying to shed its
skin out of season.

Shame can clog up your thinker and cause you to make poor
decisions or even to become paralyzed—unable to respond.
When a man is afraid of his wife, shame can cause him to shut
down and not communicate. When he's afraid he doesn't have
what it takes to raise a son or daughter, shame will cause him to
disappear to the garage, woods, golf course, or television. Shame
can lead to either lashing out (fight) or escape (flight). Both
choices can be unhealthy, and that soul-killing shame leaves
him feeling naked and afraid.

Remember this: God is the one who gave us emotions.
He gave them to us so we would know something's up in our
thinking. Emotions like fear can cause us to retreat when we
need to be moving forward—that's unhealthy fear. But there
is also healthy fear. If your little child runs out toward a busy
street, fear will cause you to run after him or her. Fear has given
people superhuman strength to lift a car off someone trapped
underneath. Healthy fear can kick us into gear. Shame and
condemnation, on the other hand, are never healthy. They are
not from God and are entirely different from guilt or conviction. Shame is what the enemy wants, leading you into hiding, rebellion, or fear-based compliance to try to feel better
about yourself. When we are truly guilty, we will sense the Holy
Spirit's conviction, which leads to repentance as it transforms

the heart and mind through God's grace. Repentance leads to joyful obedience.

One of my favorite books is *The Man-Eaters of Tsavo* by John Henry Patterson. This edge-of-your-seat thriller became the inspiration for the movie *The Ghost and the Darkness*. "The Ghost" and "the Darkness" were two male lions that stopped stalking game animals and started hunting humans instead. The pair devoured dozens of rail workers constructing the Uganda Railway near the Tsavo River. The project had to be halted because the rail workers were so terrified that many quit or refused to work until the lions were caught and killed. The predators were finally hunted down and shot by Lt. Col. Patterson, a British foreman; you can see their mounted skins in the Field Museum in Chicago.

A group of scientists discovered that those big cats weren't killing men just because they'd acquired a taste for human flesh. They found that the lion that had killed the majority of the rail workers was suffering from severe dental disease—it had an abscess in one of its canines—and its partner had also suffered injuries to its teeth and jaw. This would have made hunting healthy, strong game nearly impossible. In other words, these lions could only pick on the weak or the unhealthy.

The enemy's attacks are like the lions of Tsavo; he can only consume those who are weak, who are not finding their identity in Christ. God, who comes into the believer the moment he or she truly believes (Eph. 1:13), has no fear of the darkness or of any creature in heaven or on earth, for He is the Creator. He alone gives you your worth and value, and your "good enough" was fulfilled by Jesus's gift on the cross. He has cast your sins as far as the east is from the west—He remembers them no more—and He has put His righteousness within you. **Jesus took the rotting corpse of shame off your back when He carried the cross upon His own.**

How do we declaw the unseen enemy of shame? By putting on the armor of God through the constant renewing of our minds. When Satan attempts to silence you by using shame, you can clamp down on his neck with the Word of God. GAME OVER.

> Finally, be strong in the Lord and in his mighty power. Put on the full armor of God, so that you can take your stand against the devil's schemes. For our struggle is not against flesh and blood, but against the rulers, against the authorities, against the powers of this dark world and against the spiritual forces of evil in the heavenly realms. Therefore put on the full armor of God, so that when the day of evil comes, you may be able to stand your ground, and after you have done everything, to stand. Stand firm then, with the belt of truth buckled around your waist, with the breastplate of righteousness in place, and with your feet fitted with the readiness that comes from the gospel of peace. In addition to all this, take up the shield of faith, with which you can extinguish all the flaming arrows of the evil one. Take the helmet of salvation and the sword of the Spirit, which is the word of God. (Eph. 6:10–17)

## THE **BIG** QUESTION:

What lies are you believing that are causing shame? Declaw those lies by declaring the truth. (Example: "My wife doesn't want to have sex with me, so I must not be good enough." Truth: "My 'good enough' has nothing to do with whether my wife wants to have sex. My true worth and value don't come from her or from anyone else—they come from Christ alone!")

# The ABCs of a Man

Now I've said my ABCs—tell me what you think of me.

Some of my earliest memories are from when I was between the ages of four and six in the little mountain town of Rocky Grove, Pennsylvania. As the crow flies, our home was about a mile from where the Allegheny River and French Creek merge—the perfect place for a young boy longing for adventure. Kindergarten wasn't required in 1966, so I was placed directly in the first grade. Just weeks after school started, I landed in the hospital for nearly a month, putting me behind in school. When I returned to school just after Halloween, I was terrified when I was asked to stand up in front of the class and recite my ABCs, especially the way the teacher taught me to sing the last line: "Now I've said my ABCs—tell me what you think of me." It's not that I didn't know my ABCs; most kids know them by the age of three or four. It was because I didn't know the kids, and I was afraid how they might respond to me if I messed up the song.

I was discussing this with my wife recently and she replied, "That's funny—that's not the way I was taught the end of the song. I was taught, 'Now I've said my ABCs—next time won't you sing with me?'"

Interesting. How many of us, for generations, were taught, "Tell me what you think of me"? What was the message received and believed? *If I forget some of my ABCs or can't do them as fast as Tommy, am I not good enough? Am I a failure?* Even if that's not the way you were taught the end of that song, I have no doubt that the enemy infected you with plenty of shame, forging lies from your earliest cognitive moments to keep you on the hamster wheel of performance . . . and we all know what snakes do to hamsters.

My first-grade year is mostly a blip in my memory bank, as I spent so much of that year just catching up to the other students. Not only was I behind academically but I was also physically smaller than the other kids. My mother sent me to school a year early; she said I insisted on going because my best friend, Steve, who was six months older than I was, would be going. I'm sure my mother was trying to make the best choice and wanted Steve and me to grow up in the same class, but being behind in school *and* behind in age and size was going to bring on hardships in years to come that no one could foresee.

One thing I remember from my hospital stay was that I had to get a lot of shots—not in the arm, but, as Forrest Gump would say, in the but-tocks. I had severe pneumonia and a burst eardrum. I vividly remember being tired of having needles stuck in my bottom and refusing to let a new nurse give my shot. I begged for the older nurse who had given me all my shots to come, but she insisted that this nurse wasn't in the building. I threw a fit. The new, younger nurse wrestled me, trying to get my pajama bottoms pulled down, and eventually called in three or four other nurses to hold me down as she dropped my drawers. To this day I can still feel all the nurses' eyes on my bare butt as I screamed for my life—not just from the pain of another shot but because I was being exposed. I was naked and afraid once again in front of these creatures called women.

## Branded a Loser

I don't remember much about third grade. I remember being disappointed on my first day of class, when I discovered I wouldn't have the same fun-loving teacher I secretly had a crush on but an old maid instead. I also remember having my first real crush on a girl my age. We'll call her Holly.

Sometime that year I was sent with an older boy to clean the erasers for the chalkboard. There was an oversized closet in the hallway with two large trash cans where we'd bang the erasers together and the white chalk dust would fall into the cans. When the older boy patted me on the back telling me I was doing a good job, I thought I was special . . . until I got back to the classroom, and Holly laughed and pointed at my back. The older boy had been putting chalk dust all over me every time he patted my back, and it was covered with white rectangular marks; I felt like I'd been branded a loser. Then the whole classroom started laughing and pointing. Once again I felt naked and afraid, and this time it was in front of not only all my classmates but the girl I had a crush on too. I ran back to the hall closet saying I needed to clean off the chalk dust, but it was really to hide my humiliation and tears.

## Soaked in Urine

Fourth grade. 1969. A year that will go down in infamy.

After my third-grade year, I thought I'd left behind the old maid and the attack of the killer erasers. Really—what could be more humiliating than having chalk dust put all over you and a teacher who looked like Nanny McPhee, right? Wrong. In fourth grade, I was "blessed" with a scary female teacher who was as tall as Herman Munster, with the looks of Frankenstein's monster and the demeanor of Adolf Hitler.

For some unknown reason, this lady had it out for me. In fourth grade, the teachers would take all the students to the boys' and girls' bathrooms at the same time. One day, when she didn't see me come out in the order in which I'd gone in with a couple of other boys, she yelled for me to come out of the bathroom. When I didn't answer, she came storming in, walked over to me as I was still standing at the urinal, grabbed me by the shoulders, shook me, and told me to hurry up or I'd have to stay after school. I couldn't move—not because I was afraid of what she might do to me, but because the boys using the urinals on either side of me had decided they'd pee on my legs and shoes at the same time, catching me in a cross stream and leaving me soaked and dripping with urine. I hadn't even started to pee when the bullies hosed me, and now I had to obey my teacher or I was afraid I'd get hosed by her rage.

I sat in class crossing my legs and wiggling my feet, trying not to pee myself. Several times I begged her to let me go to the bathroom, never telling her what had happened out of my fear of the bullies. I was now not only afraid of her response but also afraid I'd pee myself in front of the class. Well, a little boy can only hold it for a "wee" bit. It happened. As I sat on the plastic seat connected to my desk, the urine seeped through my pants and formed a puddle underneath my buttocks. Luckily the recess bell rang and the whole class ran for the door— except for me. As she let the other kids go out the door, the teacher turned and shamed me again for being behind the other students. I couldn't hold it back any longer. I had to tell her—not about the two bullies who had left me standing in fear, soaked and smelling like pee, but that I'd peed my pants and didn't want anyone else to know. I begged her to let me slip out the side door of the school and run home to change, since our house was so close to the school that you could see it from our classroom. She grudgingly agreed, but only after she'd ordered me to go get paper towels and soapy water and clean off my chair.

I will never rub a dog's nose in its mess after soiling the carpet, especially if the dog wasn't let out when it needed to go.

My elementary experience wasn't all bad, but the budding belief of not being good enough changed my ABCs song to "Now I've said my ABCs, but I deserve your chalk and pee." There was a hidden pattern quietly forming deep inside of me that was already beginning to erode my soul. My worth and value were coming from whether I could stand up to bullies and from this creature called Woman. My experience left me feeling like I was nothing but a wimpy kid.

I love the book *Diary of a Wimpy Kid*, because in reality, that was me: gentle, caring, loving, meek, and mild. I like to think of myself now as being a "man's man"—which may be laughable and debatable to many—but what does that really mean, anyway? Is that a good thing or a bad thing? Is it even a real thing? Is it an authentic part of who I am, or am I just posing, like the guys at that men's retreat? Was *I* posing at the retreat? Jesus was both the Lion and the Lamb, and He was *anything but* a wimpy kid.

It's refreshing now to be able to look back and laugh at some of the stuff I went through without feeling exposed or "less than." I couldn't do that for decades, at least not until I began to understand my true identity.

Remember that kid who marked me with chalk? Well, we had two more encounters before I moved into junior high. He was a cheesehead—a Green Bay Packers fan. He'd been born in Wisconsin and would wear a Packers shirt to school almost every day. I, on the other hand, was a Steelers fan; growing up in western Pennsylvania, it was expected—almost required. I was the second-smallest kid in my class, and if I stuck out my tongue and stood sideways I looked like a zipper. But I was proud of the Pittsburgh Steelers, and I wasn't going to back down—not in front of all my classmates, and especially not in front of Holly. The bully was a year older and weighed significantly more than I did; he was the largest kid in the class.

One day in the sixth grade, when the teacher had stepped out of the room, this kid put me in a headlock in front of the class when I argued that the Steelers were better than the Packers. His pride couldn't take it; all the other kids agreed with me, and the only thing he could do was physically berate me in front of the class while the teacher was out. He quickly turned the tables from the kids laughing at him to laughing at me; it probably looked like an elephant seal playing with a herring. When he finally let me go, my head was so red I looked like a thermometer. Once I was free from his grasp, I quickly looked around the room to see who was watching. There was Holly, laughing hysterically, which, of course, left me feeling naked and afraid *again*. My worth and value were totally coming from what she and my other classmates thought of me, and in that moment, I was the wimpy kid, the proverbial ninety-eight-pound weakling.

What I didn't notice was the substitute teacher watching from the doorway who knew my parents. (Actually, I don't think there was anyone who *didn't* know my parents; both were teachers in our tiny town.) The substitute quickly reported what she'd witnessed to our teacher, and the two of us were kept after school to staple tests together for the next day's class.

Sometimes there are things in life that make you a legend, or at least an accidental hero.

As Cheesehead was putting the papers together into groups for me to staple, our argument started again, only this time there was no one there to watch my back if he decided to pop my head like a zit, and that's what was about to happen. Have you ever played "rock, paper, scissors"? Well, I added a new one to the game that day: a stapler. I discovered that stapler beats paper every time—or I should say it beats thumb. When he shoved a paper stack in front of me, along with a verbal threat, I missed the stack and accidentally stapled his thumb. Yep— clean through. I've never seen an elephant seal cry, but I did that day. Big tears. Ginormous cheese tears.

News quickly spread about what I'd done. The next day at school it was his thumb instead of my face that was red, and I was the little engine that could!

The thing is, I never told anyone it was an accident until now, writing this book.

## Growing Pains

My family was in church more than the average churchgoer. My mother was the worship leader, and my father was on the church board, taught Sunday school, and later ran sound and made recordings of the services that he'd send to widows and shut-ins who couldn't make it to church. I had really good parents—*really* good. My mother led worship and directed the choir at our church for thirty-five years and never took a penny for her labors. My father was one of the kindest men you'd ever meet—he would do anything for anyone in need. They were . . . *good*.

A little boy really doesn't want to be just "good." I mean, was that your goal as a kid—to grow up "good"? To an adventurous boy, "good" conveys the opposite of strong, daring, or masculine. Where I grew up, in a steel town along the Allegheny in western Pennsylvania, men were tough. They were men of steel—they worked in the steel mills, coal mines, and factories. They hunted, fished, drove 4x4 trucks, worked hard, got dirty (and some stayed dirty), played football and softball, chewed tobacco, and wrestled. And if you didn't follow suit, you were quickly labeled, picked on, seen as weak, and shunned by the cool kids. When I reached junior high, I was still one of the smallest kids in my class and was given the nickname "Brant the ant." My name is Brent, but that's the best the bully who gave me the nickname could come up with.

I spent most of my days after school and in the summers exploring the mountainside where we lived. That's where I came alive. It's where I learned to hear God speak to me. I didn't have to compare myself with anyone; I could be whoever I wanted to be and always be the best at it. I wore hiking boots, ragged blue jeans, and a flannel shirt, and I carried my BB gun, a pocket-knife, and a hand-drawn hunting license I pinned to my back just to prove I belonged in this wilderness environment. I might not fit in with the jocks, but I sure as shootin' could outdo any of them in the woods—at least in my mind.

My father grew up in the hills of Pennsylvania, but he was not the hunter that most men in the area were. He was smart, kind, caring, loving, wise, friendly, and never had a bad word to say about anybody. Yet because he didn't hunt, I overlooked a lot of those amazing attributes about my father when I was growing up. I wouldn't come to love and appreciate that side of him until many years later.

Many times, a boy's identity comes through his penis (and that can even carry over into manhood). I remember seeing my father's penis when I was a young boy, and to a four-foot-six kid with a six-foot-four father, he seemed—well, huge! I went to the high school where my father taught, and I would tell my fellow male classmates that my dad was very well endowed. Why did I do that? I think it was because I thought that if others believed that about him, maybe they would think the apple didn't fall far from the tree. *Hey, guys—my dad doesn't hunt, but . . .*

No, Dad didn't hunt, but he was amazing at coming along-side his son and equipping him with what he wanted or needed for his hobbies or passions. He purchased my first deer rifle for me when I was thirteen. It was a Remington 760 Gamemaster .30-06. This was not exactly the rifle most thirteen-year-olds—or even most sixteen-year-olds—would typically start with, but Dad didn't know any better (or maybe he did?).

When the other boys learned that I was carrying a .30-06 into the deer woods, there was a certain respect that came from other hunters. The boys my age were shooting something with much less kick: .30-30, .243, or .222. A kid of my small size shooting a .30-06 was like mounting the guns from the USS *Missouri* onto a paddleboat. The second time I shot that cannon, I secretly packed the entire contents of a Kleenex box underneath my shirt. Let's just say my first shot was the most accurate, as that was the only shot for quite a while that I made with my eyes open. After my first time sighting in that rifle, I was very ready to pull my shirt away from my shoulder to expose my he-man bruise to the other boys. In that culture, it was the mark of a warrior. I was learning how to pose—and the scary thing was, it was working for me and it felt good.

In the next few years, Dad would take me hunting on some of the most brutal winter days northwestern Pennsylvania could dish out. One frigid winter morning, with the wind chill at eighteen below zero, we got lost and walked for five miles wearing heavy felt-pack boots. Each boot probably weighed ten pounds, which, combined, was 25 percent of my body weight. After walking for hours, lost, freezing, and hungry, we ran into Pastor Towers, the senior pastor of our church.

He'd climbed up a very steep hillside and was seated on a huge rock, waiting for his prey to come by. I didn't know preachers killed stuff! He had sung duets with my mother in church sometimes, and back then, at least, male singers weren't exactly looked upon as "manly." At that time my cultural beliefs immediately classified him as a sissy, a wimp. Yet, there he was atop that giant rock, braving the elements, red and black flannel hanging down below his heavy winter coat, and he was carrying a .30-06.

Honestly, it was a bit confusing for me. I'd seen pictures of Jesus around the church and in my children's Bible, but they didn't look anything like Pastor Towers. There were pictures of Jesus with children sitting on His lap, or cuddling a lamb in His arms, or praying with hands folded, staring into the sky—and He was almost always wearing a white robe. Seeing my pastor clutching a rifle and decked out in hunting garb was a new image of a godly man for me. I was immediately drawn to Pastor Towers.

What children know about God comes mostly through what they know of their earthly father. If their father was mean, abusive, or emotionally or physically distant, they tend to see God as someone who is just waiting to "get them," punishing them for their wrongs (or even for no reason at all), or withholding Himself from them because they weren't good enough. Then there are those who've never known their fathers, like my wife. She grew up not knowing who her father was, if he was alive or dead, or if he'd loved her mother or just used her. That kind of situation leaves many feeling like God just created them to use them, and if they weren't letting God "use them" for His needs, they weren't good enough to be loved by Him, so they would run to the next man or woman in hopes of getting love from them instead. How could a loving God allow that to happen? Wouldn't that be setting you up? How do you love and worship a God like that? Why are there bullies? Why do people do bad things?

## Shame: The Silent Killer

Something happened to me from the time I was eight until I was twelve that I'd kept quiet, something that confused me and would cause me to look at the ground whenever a good-looking girl was in front of me all through high school and many years into adulthood.

Once a week, after supper, my mother would drop me off for my piano lesson in downtown Franklin, only a few miles from our home in Rocky Grove. The piano teacher had been widowed early and also housed a lot of college-aged girls in her very large historical home. Upon arriving, I'd sit in the large, high-backed wood chair outside the room until my teacher would call me in. As I'd sit down on the piano bench, week after week, she'd repeat the same pattern: she would go over to the large front window, close the shades, take off her shirt, sit in her chair in the corner of the room wearing nothing on top but her bra, and smoke a cigarette as I played. There was a large mirror strategically placed right above the piano in which I could see her sitting in her chair as I played. Once her cigarette was finished, she'd come over and stand right behind me in front of the mirror, then sit beside me to teach me that week's lesson—still wearing just her bra, her barely covered breasts just one foot from my face and pressed against me many times as I played. I was being taught a lesson all right, but it wasn't a piano lesson. It was shame. Shame because I noticed her breasts. Shame because I felt I couldn't tell my parents. Shame because I felt dirty and guilty for someone else's twisted actions. It would be many years before I could look directly at a woman.

I didn't tell my parents what was happening until more than a decade later. At first they didn't believe me, until my best friend, who'd taken lessons from the same teacher, told his mother the same thing. Both of us, my best friend and I, had been mysteriously muzzled through some quiet force. Shame is a silent killer.

Shame has quieted many good men and women. It has kept good men from running for office, from going into ministry or returning to it. It keeps them from being honest with their families about things that happened in their past, leaving them trying to figure out why Dad won't engage, why he won't go to church, pray with them, or hug or kiss them goodnight. The enemy has taken out so many good men, making them believe they're wimps because of a nickname or they're inherently bad because of past sins or even unhealthy thoughts or temptations they never acted on but that still cause them to feel dirty or ashamed. His goal is to cause you to lose heart. Lose your swing. Silence your voice. Emasculate the warrior within. He wants to take you out and never allow you to discover who you really are.

At what age did you begin to lose *your* swing? What happened that began to erode your belief in yourself or in others? What lies did you allow to convince you otherwise? Whatever the answers are to those questions, I'm sorry it happened to you, because that was the beginning of believing you had to achieve your "good enough."

It's time to untangle the lies and to find that one true voice created and purchased just for you—the voice the enemy tried to silence through the death of the Lamb, the Son of God. And there was silence—until the third day. Then out of the grave came a roar so powerful and so loud, the entire universe shook; a roar so fierce, the earth split; a roar so majestic, the rocks cried out in worship, in total awe at the majesty of the Conquering King. This Eternal King smashed the head of the serpent under His foot and conquered sin and death once and for all. ONCE AND FOR ALL!

You, my friend, are not a wimpy kid. What happened to you in your childhood does not define who you really are. *You are a child of the King!* It's time to get back in the game. It's time to claim the victory that's yours—to reclaim what's been lost. It's time to find your swing.

# THE **BIG** QUESTION:

What are three of the most embarrassing things that happened to you as a child that kindled feelings of deep shame? How did they contribute to you creating a mask— a false self?

# 17

# Restoring My Roar

Unhealthy Christians will not just shoot their wounded; they will drag them through the mud until they are unrecognizable.

The saffron-colored sun slipped below the horizon, bathing us in its glow as we tossed our foil-wrapped potatoes and onions onto the glowing coals of an ironwood fire. This was Africa—land of ancient storytellers. It's tradition here that when the sun sets and the hunt is over, those who have lived true life-and-death experiences on the dark continent will sometimes share stories of their greatest adventures. It's an honor to be in the presence of these great men, to be a part of a band of brothers in a land where both plants and animals can stick you—or kill you.

We were spending the night in thatched huts in Skukuza, South Africa, inside the borders of Kruger National Park. If you want to hear lions roar as the sun sets, this is the place to go. After we'd cleaned the last scraps from our plates, I threw a few more logs on the fire. As the glowing embers rose into the starlit sky, the stories began to flow like thick honey, each man taking his time, his slow crescendo leading to the pinnacle, much like that of a musical score. These were not just stories someone read in a book or saw on a "man against nature" documentary. These were stories told by the very men who had experienced them.

One story burned into my brain that night was of two former Special Forces commandos, now professional hunters, who'd been hired to track a wounded lion that had been terrorizing a village. The people in the community, not allowed to have actual ammunition to ward off lions, somehow got hold of an old muzzleloader and loaded it with rocks and beads. When the lion came at dusk in search of a meal, a man shot the lion in the stomach. He wounded it, but no one had the firepower to track and dispose of the lion. The next day, the two former SF hunters were brought in. Both men carried a .470 Nitro Express, a high-powered, double-barreled rifle, the rifle most serious hunters use when going after Africa's Big Five. Once on the blood trail, the two men spread ten yards apart, using only hand signals to communicate, moving in total stealth so as not to alert the lion of their presence.

When the blood trail they were tracking began to twist and turn, they realized the lion was onto them and was trying to throw them off course. When one hunter, crouched over the blood trail he was tracking, realized what was happening, he slowly rose and silently held up a clenched fist for his friend to see. The lion was close—*really* close—and he knew things were going to come unglued in a matter of seconds.

A full-grown male lion can run up to thirty-five miles per hour and leap up to thirty-six feet through the air. He can cover the width of a football field in just over four leaps. When a lion is about to pounce, he will often let out an audible "huff." Waiting for the lion to pounce was like waiting for bread to pop out of the toaster—times a thousand. Then it happened— a guttural huff arose from the side, and in an instant, the long grass bent as the six-hundred-pound lion went into a full sprint toward the first man. Before he could even raise his gun to shoot, the lion was in the air, mouth open and claws fully extended, ready to take down his prey as he'd done hundreds of times. Unless the other man intervened, in seconds the lion's jaws would be clamped on his friend. As the lion tore through the grass like a tsunami, the man followed the wave, swung his rifle into position, and pulled the trigger as the lion left his feet, sending a massive bullet that instantly blew through the ribcage and lungs of the airborne lion. The shot was right on target. The problem was that the force of the lion's tackle had knocked the first man backward, driving his leg off the ground and into the air along with the lion. The good news was that the lion was dead. The bad news was that the now fully expanded, mushroomed bullet had continued through the lion and blown a hole the size of a Coke bottle right through his best friend's thigh.

## Shooting Our Wounded

When we use shaming, shunning, judging, and condemning to try to "fix" someone instead of providing a grace-based process of recovery, healing, and restoration, it's like shooting them with a .470 Nitro Express, leaving them with a gaping wound, many times causing them to walk with a limp the rest of their life—if they're even able to get back on their feet again.

It is said that the Christian army is the only army that shoots their wounded. Unhealthy Christians will not just shoot their wounded; they will drag them through the mud until they are unrecognizable. Sometimes it doesn't stop there; they are then hung in effigy to remind others how it is when we get out of line.

How did you feel when you read that? Chances are it angered you for one of two reasons:

1. You're the one who's been shot.
2. You're the one who pulled the trigger.

This is a very sensitive subject.

Both shooter and victim are in great need of healing, but the one with the *deepest* wounds is probably the one doing the shooting; it is hurt people who hurt people. What the shooter is saying is, "I can't trust you, and I don't trust what God is doing in you, so *I* have to control the situation until I believe you have seen the error of your ways." Actually, they're really saying, "I don't trust God."

If the one who has been shot understands God's grace and is in a community of grace-based believers, the wound is one that God can heal if the wounded one chooses the healing path of trust and forgiveness.

The healing process starts vertically with a repenting and forgiving that happens between me and God. When I refuse to forgive someone who has sinned against me, I will remain angry and resentful. This is sin, whether it feels like it or not. Before forgiveness can be extended to the offender (horizontally), my vertical relationship with God must be made right by asking Him to forgive my ungodly response and asking the Holy Spirit to give me the strength and conviction to do what I cannot do on my own. Only then am I prepared to make things right with the other person. Likewise, when I refuse to repent to someone I've offended, I remain guilty and will (rightly) experience God's conviction. I need to repent, to get things right between myself and God before I can make them right with the one I offended. And making things right isn't just saying we're sorry. Many times it requires us to go to the one we've sinned against and ask them how what we've done has affected them. That process can bring amazing trust and love back into a broken relationship where the enemy has tried to steal, kill, and destroy.

God reveals His love for us through His Word, through His creation, and through the love of others. But when others have forsaken us and broken trust by dragging us through the mud—by gossiping, shaming, shunning, judging, or condemning—we can become callous. When we are secure in our true identity, through the love of our Father, we will discover that He uses the pain and attacks to make us stronger, less prideful, and more capable of loving like God loves.

Paul talks about this in his second letter to the church at Corinth:

> Therefore, in order to keep me from becoming conceited, I was given a thorn in my flesh, a messenger of Satan, to torment me. Three times I pleaded with the Lord to take it away from me. But he said to me, "My grace is sufficient for you, for my power is made perfect in weakness." Therefore I will boast all the more gladly about my weaknesses, so that Christ's power may rest on me. That is why, for Christ's sake, I delight in weaknesses, in insults, in hardships, in persecutions, in difficulties. For when I am weak, then I am strong. (2 Cor. 12:7–10)

The tragedy is that the one doing the shooting doesn't understand the true nature of God and will continue to lay others open with their barrage of fire until they realize their deep need of God's amazing grace and accept His unconditional love and soul-cleansing forgiveness, purchased for them through Christ's sacrifice on the cross.

I've sat across from many men, both in ministry and not, who have sobbed as they shared their stories of how they were devastated by the church after confessing their struggles. More than one shared how he had been participating in an addictions program for those struggling with porn to try to break free from the enemy's stronghold. One man in particular told me he hadn't acted out with another woman, but the tentacles of something he'd been exposed to as a child began wrapping themselves around his mind years later, when he was burned out from working long hours. When I asked what caused him to move back into his addiction after years of being clean, he explained, "In my world, everyone wants something from you. In my mind, I can pretend that the woman on the screen wants to know me, love me, and give herself to me with nothing expected in return. I just needed to feel wanted."

After meeting with another man, a former pastor, several times, I asked him if he'd ever go back into full-time ministry again. After a long pause, he lowered his head and sorrowfully said, "I don't think I ever could." Some pastors believe they can't serve anymore, because the church promoted humiliation instead of humility.

I've coached women who have also struggled with the same addiction. Some shared how they'd become addicted to porn and had become promiscuous because they just wanted to feel loved. Sexual addictions aren't limited to men; male or female, the enemy knows how to find that one weakness in our armor, then convince us that "thing" will complete us. Sin has an immediate payoff—that's why it can become addictive. And sin doesn't care about our denomination, position, age, or gender. The ultimate goal of the enemy is to fill us with shame, causing us to go into hiding. Once he has us there, he can sink his fangs deep into us, body and soul, paralyzing even the strongest believer unless those lies get untwisted by the Truth.

Sometimes our greatest pain comes from the lies we give ourselves permission to believe. It amazes me how convincingly we can *say* that there is "no condemnation for those who are in Christ Jesus" (Rom. 8:1), yet our actions show that we really believe we *should* be experiencing shame and condemnation—and from a God who sent His only Son to die for *all* of our sins! Most of us can recite John 3:16, but how many of us know John 3:17?

> For God did not send His Son into the world to condemn the world, but that the world might be saved through Him. (NASB)

If God didn't send His Son into the world to condemn (or judge) the world, then why do we think it's our job to judge or condemn others? Did I miss something? Did God somehow write in Scripture that He's given sinful people a license to judge—like a concealed carry permit, where we are allowed to pull out our spiritual gun and fire at someone we believe deserves to be shot?

## Meeting with My "Spiritual Yoda"

One day I was sitting with my friend Derek, a man who has had a huge influence on me over the past decade—discipling me week after week (sometimes daily), repeatedly walking with me through my own sin and pain and back to health. We were talking about this exact concept, where we think it's our job to fix and control others. Derek is like a "spiritual Yoda" who is able to bring revelation in a way that turns me upside down and leaves me standing there with my mouth wide open. I shared with him what I'd written here, and he used his "Jedi powers" to help me see what lay beneath the surface that I wasn't seeing.

He went back over my assertion about what those who shoot the wounded are really saying, then began unpacking and untangling the subject. "Often people feel like they have a responsibility to fix other people. The individual believes that if the other person is fixed, then the fixer will feel better. So they feel like they *need* the other person to get fixed and will do whatever it takes to fix them.

"For example, I think I need my son to 'get fixed' (say, by stopping smoking pot, or getting better grades, or going to church) so that I will look better. Then other people will think I'm a great dad, and I will feel good about my performance as a father. If my son does not 'get better,' I think it makes me look bad, so I will try to fix my son," he said. "The same thing happens in organizations—a church, for example. Say the pastor is caught using porn. Obviously, this is a problem. The sad thing is, often it is a problem *not* because we care about the pastor who is caught in the grip of porn but because it makes the organization look bad. We may threaten the sinner or attempt to control their actions by forcing them to join an accountability group, go away for intensive counseling, or attend a twelve-step recovery program. We will manipulate, humiliate, and even shun them. Why? Because we think the sinner makes the church look bad, so the church needs the person to get fixed so it can look better (and therefore feel better).

"Sometimes people recognize that individuals and organizations really have no way to fix people at all. They recognize that God is the One who causes people to grow. Look at 1 Corinthians 3:6—Paul plants, Apollos waters, but God causes the growth. So we think, 'Well, since I can't fix them, maybe God can fix them. That's what Scripture says—God will fix them!' Well, that's *not* what Scripture says. The Bible does not say God *will* fix them. The Bible says God *can* fix them, but we cannot. We twist this logic and say, 'Since I can't fix them, God will fix them. If I can't succeed in controlling or manipulating someone else to change, I'll try to get God to control and manipulate them to change. That way I (or the organization) can feel better.' But then God doesn't fix them; in fact, God sometimes actually gives them completely over to their sin and wipes His hands totally clean from them (see Rom. 1:24–25)! Now what do we do? Now we get mad at God for not fixing them, or we take back the reins and decide we will try to fix them. 'I need them to be fixed! They must be fixed!' Why? Because I need to feel better (or I think the organization needs to look better).

"What is the solution? The solution is grace. The reality is that Christians do not need to be fixed. They are *already* fixed—that's why Christ died on the cross. However, many people are scared of this solution; they think grace will make people sin more. Actually, just the opposite is the case. Let's use the example of the pastor looking at porn. Often, the reason a man looks at porn is because he is not feeling good about himself—he's under a lot of stress or is feeling worthless because his church (in the case of a pastor) is not growing fast enough. So he looks at porn to get a spike of dopamine so he can cover the feeling of being a loser. Maybe some people at his church have been critical of him, so he looks at porn and imagines that at least someone is approving of him, even if only in his imagination.

"What about the church member who drinks too much— why is he drinking? Maybe he feels like a loser because his wife does not love him anymore, so he drinks to cover the pain. The action of sin is often simply a way to mask the feeling that we are not good enough, valuable enough, or worthy enough. But the gospel says that Christ died so that you may receive the gift of righteousness (Rom. 3 and 5). In other words, when Christ comes into your life, He makes you good enough. Good enough to be loved by God. Good enough to go to heaven! *He* does that, not you. That is grace. But the pastor and the alcoholic simply forgot they were already good enough, so they sinned to mask the pain.

"So if the problem is that they felt like they weren't good enough, what is the solution? Many believe the solution to someone who sins because they feel worthless is to shun them, fire them, or even humiliate them by parading them in front of a congregation to expose the sin. It should be obvious that this would actually cause more feelings of unworthiness, thus more sin. However, imagine if the pastor and the alcoholic were reminded of who they already are. Imagine what might happen if they were reminded that, because of Christ, they have Christ's righteousness in them, they have the love of God completely enveloping them, they are completely accepted and good enough! Now what happens to the need for porn to mask the pain of unacceptance? Porn is no longer needed. Where is the need for alcohol to cover the pain of being unloved, a loser, not good enough? Gone! Sin is overcome by the power of grace!"

Boom.

Derek and I had met when I was at my absolute bottom. I was paraded in front of a congregation years ago for getting too close emotionally to a woman in the church while I was on the church staff. As a part of my "restoration" process, I was required to stand in front of twelve hundred people in three separate services and confess my sin before them. I stood there sobbing before the people I loved, feeling ashamed, isolated, and condemned. As you can imagine, I resigned shortly thereafter and spent the next several months curled up in the fetal position, wanting to die. The weight of shame was like a heavy black tar coating my body and my eyes, keeping me from being able to move or to see the light of hope. At one point it got so bad that I took my shotgun, held it to my mouth, and seriously contemplated pulling the trigger, because the shame and condemnation were unbearable.

## Listening to the Right Voices

When the opinions of others can drive us to contemplate taking our own life, we're listening to the wrong voice. I didn't need to shoot myself; others had done that for me. I had jumped through every shame-based hoop I was asked or required to in order to be restored, but none of them changed my heart; they only hardened it. The "works" I was required to do, I did shamefully, alone, and out of sight. What I desperately needed were restorative voices speaking into me, those who could remind me of my identity in Christ, not my sin. But there were no such voices speaking to me. It was as if I were a leper—"do not get close to me, do not speak to me, and absolutely do not touch me." The message communicated to me through the withholding of relationship and restoration was that my sin disqualified me from love, compassion, and even ministry. Nothing I was required to do to "keep me in check" kept me from sinning or brought me closer to God. They only drove me deeper into hiding.

After moving my family back to Indiana only a few months after my resignation, God led me to Derek. Instead of shaming, shunning, condemning, and judging, he talked to me about God's grace and how my identity was in Christ, not in my sin. His words were different. They didn't leave a nasty spiritual residue like performance-based religion did. They didn't leave me feeling not good enough. They were redemptive, healing, freeing, and restorative. The message of the gospel transformed me as I began to truly understand where my "good enough" came from. Instead of driving me into more isolation, more sin, more works-based performance, the message of God's grace created an overwhelming, unquenchable force inside of me to want to share His goodness and love. The day I limped off the church platform feeling like my spiritual legs were broken, in my anger and hurt I made a vow that I would *never* do church ministry again. But because God opened my eyes to His love and grace, I renounced that vow. As a result, I've had the opportunity to use my story—my limp—to build stronger, healthier relationships and change lives through the message of love and grace instead of condemnation. I have seen over thirteen thousand people come to Christ in just the past decade. I now know that the dark mud I was dragged through, that Satan tried to use to cover up my core identity, never had any effect on who I really was—and it never will.

The lies that come at us through the voices of those who don't understand righteousness can silence our roar. When our one, true roar is silenced, we become vulnerable—easily preyed upon. When I lose my roar, I allow myself to be shot because I believe I deserve to be attacked. Here's the truth: **My roar isn't for others to steal. What they didn't give me, they can't take away.**

Understanding God's grace alone is what restored my roar. Like the law code, those requirements only led to more fear, anger, shame, and performance-based beliefs. My sin, along with the need for others' good opinions of me, had been washed away *entirely* by the blood of the Lamb the moment I truly believed—I just didn't know it yet. But after God opened my eyes to this truth, I could no longer find the gaping bullet holes that for years kept me angry at the Christian "army," because no one has the power to undo what God sent His Son to do: to die for my sins. The power over death was cured through the blood of the only One who was without sin: Jesus. And He invites us to come to the waters to cleanse *every* sin—*once and for all.*

> God went for the jugular when he sent his own Son. He didn't deal with the problem as something remote and unimportant. In his Son, Jesus, he personally took on the human condition, entered the disordered mess of struggling humanity in order to set it right once and for all. The law code, weakened as it always was by fractured human nature, could never have done that.
>
> The law always ended up being used as a Band-Aid on sin instead of a deep healing of it. And now what the law code asked for but we couldn't deliver is accomplished as we, instead

of redoubling our own efforts, simply embrace what the Spirit is doing in us. (Rom. 8:3–4 MSG)

## THE **BIG** QUESTION:

Is there a sin from your past that you believe you should feel shame and condemnation for? What does God's Word say about that?

# 18

# Counted as Warriors

We must create a place so safe that men can share, cry, and grieve, and still be counted as warriors.

A ge is something that creeps up on us, like a hunter stalking his prey. But as the steam on Father Time's mirror clears, we begin to see ourselves more clearly and a subtle shift begins in our core, letting us know we are on borrowed time. We begin to think about things like *Do I have enough money for retirement?* or *What if something happened to me— would there be enough left to take care of my spouse and kids? How should my belongings be distributed? Did I accomplish the purpose for which I was put on this earth?* And most importantly, *What kind of a legacy did I leave—did I love well?* I've heard it said that wrinkles should merely indicate where your smiles have been.

That's true, but reality is that, while in this life we will have joys, we will also face hardships and loss—deep, soul-wrenching loss.

I had stepped into the kitchen for no more than five minutes to fix a sandwich when my father passed. I had stayed by his side for five days straight—singing to him, telling stories, playing music, praying, holding his paralyzed hand—and he goes and dies when I step away for a few minutes? Really? I know there are many who don't get to spend that kind of time with a loved one as they're passing, but honestly, I felt robbed at first. Why couldn't I be there when he took his final breath? Before I left his bedside to go to the kitchen, I said, "When Jesus comes to take your hand and calls you by name, it's okay to go. I'll make sure Mom's taken care of." And within a few minutes, he was gone. It was as if he'd been waiting for the assurance that Mom would be taken care of before he finally let go. That is exactly how my dad was with my mom—he always did everything he could for her. Dad loved well.

What children know about God almost always comes through their earthly fathers. I knew Dad was in a much better place after he'd passed, but inside I was dying. I held it together, and even tried to convince myself that it was "well with my soul." And in one way it was—I knew my dad was in heaven and that I would see him again. But I had just lost my best friend—my father— the one who'd been my representation of God through my entire life. The final page had been turned, and the book was now shut. The end. There was a peace knowing where he now was, but there was also a void wider than the Grand Canyon that could not be filled. I felt as if all my strength—*all* of it—was taken from me. Now who would I call to talk to about the weather, the Steelers, how to fix things, my job, my relationships; to brag about my kids; to discuss vacation plans or where we'll spend the holidays? Privately, the tears were coming from a deeper place than I'd ever cried before. It was as if my soul was a sponge and every drop inside had been squeezed out. I felt empty. A son wants his father to be proud of him, to know he's enough in his father's eyes. When a man loses his father, that's when his biggest question rings the loudest: *Was my father proud of me? Did he see me as having what it takes to be a man?*

## Wounded Warriors

The most moving scene around this topic is from my all-time favorite movie, *Braveheart*. A father and son, Campbell and Hamish, have been fighting side by side in a brutal battle, and the father has been mortally wounded. Campbell's final words have stuck with me ever since the first time I saw the movie. Knowing his son needs the affirmation that every son needs from his father, Campbell says, "I've lived long enough to live free, proud to see you become the man you are. I'm a happy man."[1] What an amazing gift those words were to his son! As Campbell slumps forward in death, Hamish presses his head against his father's and begins to weep. In the background, William Wallace and a fellow warrior, Stephen, look on with an expression on their faces that is hard to describe—it's something that can only be experienced, and it guts you like you've been opened up with a dull knife. The warriors in that scene all have war paint on their faces and wounds from the battle, but those wounds are small compared to the wound Hamish is now feeling. In that moment, nothing else matters. Nothing.

As I watched that scene, the tears began to pour like rain. It hit me in a spot where nothing else can touch me, a place reserved only for my relationship with my father. Maybe you didn't have a healthy relationship with your father. Maybe you hated your father (and maybe you still do). Maybe you didn't have a father in your life at all. No matter what, you have a father wound, or you will at some point, because there has only ever been one perfect Father. And in the moments when your anger, hurt, and deep sadness strike, you will want to run away and hide. It's a grief that you can't deny, cover up, or wish away, and that pain will wound you like nothing else. You will feel like no one understands what you are going through; no matter who is there with you, you'll feel like you are in this alone.

Viewing that moving scene triggered something deep inside me and took me to a very dark place. I had been feeling down for several months but had been trying to cover my tracks— those shameful thoughts of feeling like a failure. I'd wanted just a few more years with my father so he could see me complete my book and have it picked up by a major publisher and found in bookstores nationwide. I wanted him to smile at me and say the words, "I'm so proud of you, son." The funny thing is, he'd done that many times in my life, so why did I feel like I still needed that affirmation? Was it really him I was needing it from, or was I yearning to experience sonship with my heavenly Father?

Several years ago, a movie called *The Heart of Man* was released in which a dear friend and mentor of mine acted. It's a powerful story of a son who leaves his loving father's side, where everything was good, to indulge his sexual lust for women. The only thing that saves the man is the love of his father, who, although he knows the sin his son is going to commit, never stops loving him, never gives up on him, never forsakes him. *Never.*

There is a participant's guide for the movie, and in it, Timothy Keller tells a story that really put what I was feeling into perspective:

> There's an old story by Thomas Goodwin, a 17th-century Puritan pastor. . . . One day Goodwin was taking a walk and saw a father and son walking along the street. Suddenly the father swept the son up into his arms and hugged him and kissed him and told the boy he loved him—and then, after a minute, he put the boy back down. Was the little boy more a son in the father's arms than he was down on the street? Objectively and legally there was no difference, but subjectively and experientially, there was all the difference in the world. In his father's arms, the boy was experiencing his sonship.
>
> This was an assurance of who this little boy was. The love of God enables us to say to ourselves, "If someone as all-powerful as that loves me like this, delights in me, has gone to infinite lengths to save me, says he will never let me go, and is going

to glorify me and make me perfect and take everything bad out of my life—if all of that is true—why am I worried about anything?" At a minimum this means joy, and a lack of fear and self-consciousness.[2]

What I was longing for was more than just my father's pat on the back, an "Attaboy" or "Go get 'em, son!" I was needing his touch, and I knew that was forever gone in this life.

When my father fought his first battle with cancer, he shared a hospital room with another man. While sitting at the foot of Dad's bed, I saw his roommate's sixty-something son crawl up into bed beside his ailing father. I was only thirty-five at the time and couldn't truly comprehend what I was seeing. Now I do. That father and son had a closeness most people in this world can't fathom, and I was gifted a holy moment to witness what God intends for us to experience—His undying love. The son was trying to comfort his dying father, but the gift came when the father put his frail arms around his son and with a weak voice whispered, "I love you, son."

My father had a massive stroke five days before he passed and was unable to even blink, let alone raise his arms or speak. I knew Dad was conscious of what was going on around him, because when I'd talk about adventures we'd taken together, how I was thankful to have experienced them with him and what he meant to me, a tear would roll down his cheek. I knew my words had touched him deeply, but I didn't realize until I was writing this chapter that his tears could have also been his only way of communicating to me what he was so desperately wanting to say: "Son, I love you, and I'm proud to see you become the man you are." I held my dad's hand more in the final days of his life than I had since I was a little boy. I experienced sonship with my father.

As I said, the loss of a father can leave you in a very dark place. It's not something that can be fixed; it has to be grieved— worked through—and it can take you to the edge of a cliff.

## Unearthing the Lies

At our church's Christmas Eve service, the pastor asked the congregation to write down the false names the enemy had been calling us. After taking communion, we were instructed to take those pieces of paper, tear them up into little pieces, and scatter them all over the floor at the front of the church. I wrote down two short phrases I'd been unknowingly believing about myself. The first was "warning track power." When I was a boy playing ball, the other boys would shout that phrase as I stepped up to the plate, implying that I didn't have enough power to hit one over the fence, so I'd be an easy out. The second falsehood I was believing about myself was "not good enough." I knew in my head that these names were not coming from God, but deep inside they were attached to me like Velcro—I couldn't shake them off.

That evening, Stacy and I went out for dinner, then came home to an empty house—the children in our blended family were at their other parents' homes. It was a lonely feeling. As I sat at the table, I felt a drop of water hit my arm, and then another. Great—not only had the toilet flooded and water had begun to come through the ceiling, but it was the second time this had happened in six months. As if the day needed more drama, that flooded bathroom began a flood in my thoughts that eventually swept over me and washed me right to the edge of the cliff. There was no space left in my tank to put any more hard stuff, and the unhealthy thoughts and feelings inside of me began spilling over the edges.

By the time Christmas night arrived, what I'd been fighting hard to hide was now being exposed. Others began to realize something was up and started asking what was wrong. I answered with half-truths: "I'm sad because my parents aren't here," and, "I'm having a hard time because the kids are at their other parents' houses." But that was not the whole story. The real truth was that the enemy's lies were beginning to explode, and I couldn't stuff them down any longer. Why was this happening? Why did I feel this way? I had been either too proud or too afraid to confront the thoughts and feelings that had been growing in my mind like a cancer.

On December 26, I could no longer contain what was erupting inside of me. I went upstairs to the bedroom, shut the door, and opened the top drawer of my dresser. I keep a number of things in there, among them a pen and paper, a copy of *The Heart of Man Participant's Guide*, and a .44 Magnum handgun. As I reached for the pen and paper to start writing down my thoughts, the enemy shot me with one of his flaming arrows the second my eyes caught the .44 Mag. I snuffed out that arrow and proceeded to take out the pen, paper, and participant's guide, and opened the guide. Here are the words on the opening page:

> The journey of *The Heart of Man* that you are being invited to is not for the faint of heart. Being honest with yourself takes profound bravery, and sharing your darkness with others can be terrifying. We encourage you to be brave. Be courageous. Healing, hope, and power are waiting for you.[3]

I wrote on the first paper: "Being honest with yourself takes extreme bravery. Be brave." As Doc Holliday said in the movie *Tombstone*, "No, make no mistake; it's not revenge he's after—it's a reckoning."[4] This was a moment I'd been dodging for a long, long time. Being this kind of honest with myself was going to take more than being brave; it meant I had to *trust God completely*. It was time for me to write down all the false names that the enemy had been calling me—all the false narratives, all the lies I'd been believing. As I began putting pen to paper, I was drawing from a place I had never given myself permission to go. This was the reckoning. I knew that if I took this list of thoughts to almost anyone I knew, they would either try to fix me or commit me. Yet if I needed to be committed, I needed to know it. That's a really scary thing to say out loud. But I was trusting God with everything now, maybe for the first time in my life.

Here are my thoughts in order as they came out on paper:

- I feel hopeless.
- I feel friendless.
- I feel trapped in this life.
- I'm totally numb and trust no one.
- I'm afraid I will never be good enough.
- It's too late for me to do anything with my life.
- I feel worthless because I don't have a big enough ministry platform.
- I feel disqualified from ministry because I'm divorced.
- I believe I'm a disappointment to God.
- I believe I'm a disappointment to my wife, my kids, my family, and to others.
- I'm afraid of dying alone.
- Because I'm divorced, I'm afraid others see my heart as bad.
- I can't help others when I'm empty inside. It's being deceitful.
- I must not be worthy of others' love and caring or they would move toward me.
- I can't please anyone.
- Who would care if I died?
- I want to give up. Life is exhausting me.

- I don't believe I make a difference in anyone's life.
- I feel abandoned.
- I feel like I'm losing it.
- I hate myself.
- I'm afraid of myself.
- I hate my life.
- I'm scared because I no longer want to try to claw myself out of this hole. I secretly wish it would just cave in.
- Dying is the only solution.

As I wrote that last phrase down, the door opened and my wife walked in. The sun had set and the room was beginning to darken as she sat near the window across from me, and I began reading to her what was on those papers. When I disclosed that the enemy had tried to get me to do more than glance at the .44 Mag, her expression held both anger and fear. I knew inside that shooting myself was nothing I would ever do, but this list was enough to cause anyone to be worried. Here I was, an ordained pastor and professional life coach, and I was struggling with unhealthy thoughts and feelings so heavy that an elephant couldn't carry them on its back. Now that my struggle was out in the open, the biggest thing I was worried about was how others would respond to it. Being honest with yourself and others takes more than just bravery; it takes *fully trusting God with your whole self*.

Here's the thing: there's almost always a little truth mixed in with the enemy's lies. That's how he gets us to buy into them in the first place. The only arrow the enemy fired at me that contained absolutely zero truth was that dying was the only solution; all the other thoughts I wrote down in my list contained a small amount of truth, even if it was just how I was *feeling*. But at their core, they were all built on a lie. The lies weren't coming from the real me—Christ in me—but from Satan, the father of lies.

Satan tried to push Jesus Himself to the edge by tempting Him to believe lies—he even used Scripture to do it! But Jesus was able to defang the enemy and neutralize his poisonous lies with the Word of God.

Then Jesus was led by the Spirit into the wilderness to be tempted by the devil. After fasting forty days and forty nights, he was hungry. The tempter came to him and said, "If you are the Son of God, tell these stones to become bread."

Jesus answered, "It is written: 'Man shall not live on bread alone, but on every word that comes from the mouth of God.'"

Then the devil took him to the holy city and had him stand on the highest point of the temple. "If you are the Son of God," he said, "throw yourself down. For it is written:

'He will command his angels concerning you,
and they will lift you up in their hands,
so that you will not strike your foot against a stone.'"

Jesus answered him, "It is also written: 'Do not put the Lord your God to the test.'"

Again, the devil took him to a very high mountain and showed him all the kingdoms of the world and their splendor. "All this I will give you," he said, "if you will bow down and worship me."

Jesus said to him, "Away from me, Satan! For it is written: 'Worship the Lord your God, and serve him only.'"

Then the devil left him, and angels came and attended him. (Matt. 4:1–11)

Attempting to get Jesus to sin was the enemy's way of trying to get Him to pick up a .44 Mag and end the suffering—not by killing Himself per se, but by relinquishing His deity and giving Satan authority over Himself. But Jesus didn't give in to the lies of the enemy. He fought back—not by trying harder but by firing missiles straight from the Word of God at Satan's lies, knocking those flaming arrows out before they could land and do damage. The enemy couldn't get me to end my life by blowing my brains out, so he tried to get me to lose hope and give up.

There are times when all the renewing of your mind you can do and all the scriptural prescriptions you can come up with don't fix the problem. You find yourself on a cliff, and the only thing keeping you from going over the edge is trusting God— trusting that God is who He says He is, and *trusting that you are who God says you are*.

## Tossing the Lies off the Cliff

The following day I reached out to my close friend and pastor, Keith, to let him know what was happening with me, not because he needed to know but because I needed to throw the lies—not myself, but the lies—over the cliff by verbalizing and unpacking them with someone I trusted. The two of us spent about an hour and a half on the phone discussing my list, distinguishing between the actual lies and the crumbs of truth mixed in.

The first thing I had written down was, "I feel hopeless." Feeling hopeless wasn't the lie; that was just a feeling. The lie was that I *should* feel hopeless—that there was a reason to feel hopeless—that I *was* hopeless. But *why* did I feel that way? Because I wasn't making the money I thought I should be making at my age, I'd been through a divorce, I was hurting, my kids were hurting, some people close to me had turned their backs on me, and more. The man-killing leopard of shame was stalking me. I had been getting my "good enough"—my sense of worth—from the wrong places, and was left feeling hopeless when those things or people didn't deliver. The truth is that my hope is in the resurrected Christ. *He is my hope.* I never need to feel hopeless.

Replacing the lies with truth gets rid of the lies, but in order to really heal, we also need to grieve the very real losses tangled in with the lies. I needed to grieve the loss of some relationships that had been important to me. I understood that it was the lies *they* were buying into that had caused these people to abandon me, but that didn't stop the reality that they had gossiped about and shunned me. Those things hurt deeply. The loss of those relationships needed to be grieved.

Too many times we can be quick to tell someone to "get over it and move on." Or we give them scriptural prescriptions and

tell them to take two in the morning and it'll be fine. What a dis-
service we do to others when we don't allow them to be picked
up by their heavenly Father, hugged, kissed, told how much they
are loved, and allowed to grieve in His loving arms. Our heavenly Father invites us to share our pain with Him, to cry on His
shoulder. Even the mighty warriors in *Braveheart* could see the
pain Hamish was experiencing and allowed him the space to cry,
to feel the depth of his emotions and still be counted as a warrior.

**We must create a place so safe that men can share, cry,
and grieve and still be counted as warriors.** I know what
many of you are thinking. *C'mon, Brent—men don't feel the
need to be safe, do they? And what's this about men sharing,
crying, and grieving? Where's that in the **manual**?* Somehow,
many of us missed the memo that it's okay—not only okay, but
*necessary*—to share, to cry, and to grieve. Most males struggle
with sharing what's happening in our lives, and we're certainly
not going to cry about it—or at least, we're not going to let
anybody *see* us crying. But then how do we deal with grief?

Grief can go so deep, it's a gutting of the soul. You don't argue
with grief. If you truly want to find your way out of grief, you
have to drink that cup. First, you have to acknowledge your
sadness—your deep sorrow—as you look at the cup of grief
before you. As you pray and spend time with the Father, ask
God for the strength to embrace that cup, to let yourself fully
feel the grief. Finally, you have to trust God and drink it—all of
it. God wants to heal every ounce of your grief, no matter how
deep. But you need to work through it in order to fully heal.

Then Jesus went with his disciples to a place called Gethsemane, and he said to them, "Sit here while I go over there and pray." He took Peter and the two sons of Zebedee along with him, and he began to be sorrowful and troubled. Then he said to them, "My soul is overwhelmed with sorrow to the point of death. Stay here and keep watch with me."

Going a little farther, he fell with his face to the ground and prayed, "My Father, if it is possible, may this cup be taken from me. Yet not as I will, but as you will."

Then he returned to his disciples and found them sleeping. "Couldn't you men keep watch with me for one hour?" he asked Peter. "Watch and pray so that you will not fall into temptation. The spirit is willing, but the flesh is weak."

He went away a second time and prayed, "My Father, if it is not possible for this cup to be taken away unless I drink it, may your will be done."

When he came back, he again found them sleeping, because their eyes were heavy. So he left them and went away once more and prayed the third time, saying the same thing.

Then he returned to the disciples and said to them, "Are you still sleeping and resting? Look, the hour has come, and the Son of Man is delivered into the hands of sinners. Rise! Let us go! Here comes my betrayer!" (Matt. 26:36–46)

Jesus didn't just get away for a few minutes to ask His Father for help with His deep grief and for strength as He knew what lay before Him. His prayers were so long that the disciples kept falling asleep. And it wasn't just a one-time deal; Jesus went away to pray and grieve before His Father three times. Jesus trusted His Father enough to repeatedly pray that not His own will but the Father's will would be done. When the hour came for His betrayal, the Son of Man could trust and obey. He'd spent time with His Father, and He trusted His sonship with Him.

God promises to never leave you nor forsake you, and He doesn't care about the hour, for He neither sleeps nor slumbers, and you are a child of the King. As Tim Keller tweeted, "The only person who dares wake up a king at 3:00 AM for a glass of water is a child. We have that kind of access."[5]

Just as Campbell gave Hamish words of sonship, Jesus's Father gave Him words of sonship when He was baptized:

> As soon as Jesus was baptized, he went up out of the water. At that moment heaven was opened, and he saw the Spirit of God descending like a dove and alighting on him. And a voice from heaven said, "This is my Son, whom I love; with him I am well pleased." (3:16–17)

God wants us to take our sorrows and troubles to Him. It's more than just laying them at His feet; it's knowing we can ask the King for a drink of water at any hour, for we have that kind of access. So let it out, dear friend—*all* of it. Crawl up into His lap, and let Him hold you. Let Him rock you. Let Him speak words of sonship into your ear. Know in the depth of your soul that He delights in you! Trust Him, and allow Him to be the safe place where you can share, cry, and grieve and still be counted as the warrior that you are.

## THE **BIG** QUESTION:

The enemy of your soul doesn't want you to understand your sonship with God—that you are His beloved. If you did, he knows you would be dangerous to him. The devil, your enemy, "prowls around like a roaring lion looking for someone to devour" (1 Pet. 5:8). My friend, as a believer, you have the *Lion of Judah* in you! What will you say to your enemy right now to let him know that no matter what he throws at you, you understand who and whose you really are, and you're not going to back down?

# 19

# Recognizing the Roar Within

Some people can be so disoriented to God that when
he begins to work around them, they actually become
annoyed at the interruption!

HENRY T. BLACKABY

I have always loved nature and animals, and stories having
to do with them. There is a legend about a flock of geese
that saved a city. An enemy army planned to invade a
Roman city and sent stealthy attackers in the dark of the night,
but as they approached the city, a sacred flock of geese were
awakened and alerted the Roman guards. The Roman army
turned back the invaders, and the geese went down in history
as saving Rome. Geese watch at night and give warning with
their noise. A flock of wild geese is always watching.

## Chasing the Wild Goose

Interestingly, the ancient Celtic people saw the Holy Spirit not as a hovering white dove as many of us now do, but as a wild goose. The meaning behind this choice of birds is that they saw how the Holy Spirit has a tendency to surprise and disrupt. The Holy Spirit moves in our lives in an unexpected fashion, similar to the actions of a wild goose. This is constantly reflected in the lives of biblical characters, who often had their own ideas regarding how they would follow God but were then led in an unexpected way by the Holy Spirit.

How do we know when the voice of God is speaking to us? John 10:27 says, "My sheep hear My voice, and I know them, and they follow Me" (NASB). In my life, the thing that has caused me to pause, listen, and obey came through the door of my emotions. There was an emotional alert that I recognized in my spirit. That is key when discerning the voice of the Holy Spirit.

## God's Invisible Dog Fence

When I'm teaching small groups about discerning if what we're hearing is God's voice, the enemy's voice, or just last night's double pepperoni pizza, I use a diagram I've dubbed "God's Invisible Dog Fence." In each group, there's almost always at least one person who has an invisible dog fence. When I ask why they installed it, they always reply that it's to keep the dog contained so it won't get hurt. They put a collar on the dog that will beep as the dog gets closer to the invisible fence; the closer it gets, the more intense the beeping becomes. What happens if the dog ignores the beep and goes even closer to the boundary? "It gets shocked," is the uneasy reply, as if the owner is the one responsible for hurting the dog. When I ask why they would use a device that could cause pain, they always—*always*—reply that it's because they love the dog. They know that once their dog learns to recognize the beeps, it can avoid pain by simply turning around. Next, I ask, "What do you do if your dog makes a poor choice, breaks through the invisible fence, and gets zapped? Do you run down there and kick the dog, calling it derogatory names?" The incredulous look on their face at that point illustrates their love for their dog—they would *never* do that! They would go to the dog, take it back to where it's safe, and walk it around the perimeter to reinforce where it's okay to go. The dog knows the voice of its master, and knows it is loved.

Since the very beginning of time, God has had a boundary for His children that lets them know where it's safe to go and where it isn't. The boundaries are charged like an electric fence with the lies of the enemy, who always mixes a little truth in with his lies to try to entice us to go where we'd *never* go if we were thinking clearly. The closer the believer gets to what's not good for them (the more lies they're buying into), the more his or her emotions will begin to become unhealthy—emotions like lust, jealousy, envy, hate, anger, rage, guilt, and so on. These emotions line up with the deeds of the flesh listed in Galatians 5:19–21.

Emotions, in and of themselves, aren't bad; God gave them to us to let us know if we are headed in the right or wrong direction—like a beeper collar. When we cross His boundary and the unhealthy emotions lead us into sin, there are negative consequences. As long as we continue in what's not good for us, we will continue to have negative consequences. Those consequences have nothing to do with our salvation; for the believer, sin is a maturity issue, not a salvation issue. God does not remove our salvation from us because we make a poor choice and get zapped.

When we are within the boundaries of where God created for us to live, we experience healthy emotions that line up with the fruit of the Spirit (Gal. 5:22–23): love, joy, peace, patience, kindness, goodness, faithfulness, gentleness, and self-control. Even some "difficult" emotions have a healthy version. We've talked about healthy fear (a child runs toward a busy street and healthy fear gives you the energy you need to run and rescue them) and righteous anger (you see someone being assaulted and righteous anger causes you to intervene to protect them). It's crucial to be able to discern the difference between healthy and unhealthy emotions.

## Treat Them Gently

The sad thing is that many Christians don't trust God's boundaries for others, so with what they think are good intentions, they attempt to control someone headed in an unhealthy direction, trying to get them to change their behaviors. As mentioned earlier, they will do this through humiliating, shunning, judging, or shaming—trying to guilt a person into obedience. If you're the one doing that to others, let me ask you: How's that working out?

I love the entire chapter of Romans 14. It helps us understand what to do when a person isn't seeing truth clearly and is making what seems to us to be senseless mistakes or is outright sinning. I really like the way *The Message* puts it:

> Welcome with open arms fellow believers who don't see things the way you do. And don't jump all over them every time they do or say something you don't agree with—even when it seems that they are strong on opinions but weak in the faith department. Remember, they have their own history to deal with. Treat them gently. (Rom. 14:1 MSG)

Romans 14:4 drives home the truth that *God* is the one who calls the shots by saying, "If there are corrections to be made or manners to be learned, God can handle that without your help" (MSG). This isn't to say that we as believers don't have a place in helping someone headed in the wrong direction. But unless we have a healthy track record with them and/or have permission to speak into the dark and painful places in their life, we don't have the right to do that. In that case, our job as a brother (or sister) in Christ is to sincerely pray for them.

Sometimes we don't recognize when we are getting too close to things that could be harmful to us—we don't hear the beeps on our collar—because we've never been taught how to untangle the lies twisted up in our thoughts, creating unhealthy emotions. We remain tyrannized by lies we didn't even know we believed, and the unhealthy emotions resulting from them can cause us to get zapped when we move in the direction of the enemy's lies and cross the boundary into sin.

What are we to do when we start hearing the beeping of unhealthy emotions in our head? We need to think like Christ. We have to take those unhealthy thoughts captive, then replace the lies we're believing with God's truth. Once we have broken through the fence, it's not safe. In order to stay safe and healthy and mature in our faith, we have to get rid of the lies that cause us to want to get too close or to break through the invisible fence.

> The world is unprincipled. It's dog-eat-dog out there! The world doesn't fight fair. But we don't live or fight our battles that way—never have and never will. The tools of our trade aren't for marketing or manipulation, but they are for demolishing that entire massively corrupt culture. We use our powerful God-tools for smashing warped philosophies, tearing down barriers erected against the truth of God, fitting every loose thought and emotion and impulse into the structure of life shaped by Christ. Our tools are ready at hand for clearing the ground of every obstruction and building lives of obedience into maturity. (2 Cor. 10:3–6 MSG)

We have to learn to think like Christ and trust that He knows what's best for us when we want to stray into sin. Remember, sin always has an immediate payoff—that's why it's so attractive. In order for us not to covet what's on the other side of the fence that we think we need, we have to know and trust that we have the unconditional love of our Master, and that our Master knows and always does what is best for us.

That's where we can be a guide—through loving others the way God loves us.

Do we speak truth when necessary? Of course—but only when we are sure that the Holy Spirit is leading us to do it. That green light from God will only come when we are free of any agenda of our own and free of pride and self-righteousness. We must be careful not to create a smaller perimeter than God has set by trying to fix or control the individual (thinking that *we* in our own wisdom know what is best for that person), and it should always be done in a way that leads the person to their own "Aha!" moment. We want them to be able to recognize the voice of the Holy Spirit; if we use shame to get them to do what *we* think is best, *we* have now become the voice they are listening to. We may even be squelching the voice of the Spirit, which will only lead them into more unhealthy choices.

Sometimes, in our nearsightedness, we find it difficult to recognize when the Holy Spirit is bringing an opportunity to us to be a part of another's healing. We can become so focused on ourselves and our own agenda that we miss what God is doing. In the book *Hearing God's Voice*, Henry Blackaby states, "Some people can be so disoriented to God that when he begins to work around them, they actually become annoyed at the interruption!"[1] We feel inconvenienced if someone who is struggling comes to us for guidance and help. In our own unhealthiness, we listen merely to correct them instead of listening in order to hear their heart and story. When we do that, there is no room for the direction of the Holy Spirit, because we believe *we* know what's best for the other person. When we leave out the guidance of the Holy Spirit, we have taken on the role of judge, jury, and corrections officer, manhandling the handcuffed offender into solitary confinement using guilt, shame, condemnation, and judgment. I've seen how this can get ugly.

A number of years ago, a friend of mine, an amazing studio musician living in Nashville, was playing piano and touring across the country with a number of major-label Christian artists. When many churches stopped bringing in expensive tours because they had their own talented praise and worship teams, the touring began to dry up and he found himself unable to make the money needed to support his family. He began playing with several local club bands, which took him to a number of venues with drinking, women, flirting—you get the idea. His wife, who struggled with needing control, tried to create an even smaller fence around him than God did by attempting to dictate where, when, and with whom he could play. She also let him know that he was not allowed to talk to women at these events and must text him as soon as the band was done playing to let her know exactly when she should expect him home. Do you think he stayed inside the box she created for him? He didn't; he had an affair, which resulted in divorce. In this situation, all the big five man-killers (lack of purpose, disrespect, anger, lust, and shame) took down his marriage.

Now, my friend made his own unhealthy choices. He *chose* to sin—he was 100 percent responsible for his own actions. But his wife also sinned. Because of her own fears and insecurities, she tried to control him, to take the place of the Holy Spirit. Whose voice do you think she was trying to get him to follow more—hers or God's? One would lead merely to conformity, and one would lead to repentance. Conformity does not bring about a true change of heart and can actually give rise to rebellion.

One of the most disturbing things about the whole situation was that several Christian producers he'd played for in the studio blacklisted him out of anger. Because of his sin, they shunned him—they wouldn't hire him. He became the topic of their gossip and slander; as a result, my friend struggles to this day with setting foot inside a church or trusting anyone who claims to be a Christian. It was legalistic judgment that caused them to shun him and attempt to keep him from coming back inside the fence. What they didn't realize is that, living in their own arrogant sins of anger, judgment, and unforgiveness, they were on the other side of the fence as well and had caused spiritual harm to him and anyone else witnessing their behavior. The way they treated him was like a predator—they clamped down on him, shutting off his ability to live. That's what man-killers do when finishing off their prey. Those who should have been *praying for* him were now *preying on* him.

Their consequence is that until they forgive, they'll remain angry and judgmental, locking themselves in a kennel instead of running freely in God's big yard of grace. The truth of the gospel is that God wants all of us to flourish inside the boundary of His unconditional love through His mercy and grace, made possible when He sent Jesus to die in our place.

A great illustration of this is found in the story Jesus told of the prodigal son.

> Now his older son was in the field, and when he came and approached the house, he heard music and dancing. And he summoned one of the servants and began inquiring what these things could be. And he said to him, "Your brother has come, and your father has killed the fattened calf because he has received him back safe and sound." But he became angry and was not willing to go in; and his father came out and began pleading with him. But he answered and said to his father, "Look! For so many years I have been serving you and I have never neglected a command of yours; and yet you have never given me a young goat, so that I might celebrate with my friends; but when this son of yours came, who has devoured your wealth with prostitutes, you killed the fattened calf for him." And he said to him, "Son, you have always been with me, and all that is mine is yours. But we had to celebrate and rejoice, for this brother of yours was dead and has begun to live, and was lost and has been found." (Luke 15:25–32 NASB)

The older son was "the good son"—the son who never got in trouble, obeyed all the rules, and believed he was entitled to all his father had because of his compliance with his father's wishes. This son believed he should be able to call the shots against his younger brother and demanded his inheritance from his father because of his compliance. His own anger, jealousy, judgment, and feelings of entitlement kept him from being able to recognize the voice of a loving father. It was the older brother's self-righteous pride that kept him from the party; it was the same self-righteous pride of the producers that tried to keep my friend in Nashville from being hired.

It is easier for a man who's been broken to humbly return with open hands and an open heart and learn to walk again than it is for the self-righteous man to bow down, unclench his fists, and learn to crawl again.

One son was repentant, and one was prideful. Which one did the father invite to the party? He invited *both*! This scandalous grace is offensive to some, but to others, it is so sweet that it brings them to repentance. "Or do you think lightly of the riches of His kindness and tolerance and patience, not knowing that the kindness of God leads you to repentance?" (Rom. 2:4 NASB).

## The Scandalous Feast

Jesus performed His first miracle at a wedding reception, turning several large containers of water into wine. John said that this miracle was a sign of what His ministry would be about. Jesus came to bring *festival joy* to you and me, His bride. He secured a "not guilty" verdict for us so we are no longer liable for our sins. If you just read this, furrowed your brow, and found it necessary to add, "Yes, but we still have consequences," you just might be afraid that God's grace and freedom are too good to be true. If that's the case, you need to lighten up, Francis—you have a reason to party! The Bible tells us to "taste and see that the LORD is good" (Ps. 34:8). Our God wants us to experience His goodness, to know that He would actually throw a feast for us because He loves us so much. Once you begin to recognize His voice, you will want to accept the invitation to His table—and be a part of setting it for others who are hungering and thirsting for His love, understanding, and compassion.

Theologian Jonathan Edwards explains, "The difference between believing that God is gracious, and tasting that God is gracious is as different as having a rational belief that honey is sweet, and having the actual sense of its sweetness."[2] Unless our theology touches our reality, we have never tasted the Lord's goodness. The absence of His sweetness in our hearts causes us to speak out with a bitter tongue toward others and robs us of our joy.

What if we believed that repentance wasn't a gift from us to God but actually a gift from God to us? The father in the prodigal son story didn't wait for his son to crawl back but *ran* to him when he saw him coming. According to the law, the son should have been cast out not just from the father's house but from the entire community. His heavenly Father gave the wayward son the gift of repentance, then his earthly father gave him the gift of forgiveness when he didn't deserve it and threw him the feast of all feasts.

The salvation Jesus provided for us is a feast. When you understand and experience in your heart that Jesus set the table for you when you didn't deserve it, your theology will touch your reality, and you will taste His amazing grace. That the Father actually *runs* to His children when we call out, breaks through the invisible fence, picks us up, forgives us, never disowns us, teaches us once again where the healthy boundaries are, and then throws an amazing feast for us is absolutely scandalous. When we believe in and rest in His work for us, He becomes real to our hearts. God wants us to taste His goodness on the palate of our hearts like a wine taster savors the flavor of a rare vintage in his or her mouth, and He desires for us to find our refuge and strength in Him. It's only by tasting and listening that we begin to recognize the roar within—the beautiful voice of the Holy Spirit, conquering our fear of darkness as we learn to take refuge in Him.

> Taste and see that the LORD is good;
>    blessed is the one who takes refuge in him. (34:8)

## THE **BIG** QUESTION:

The prodigal son discovered that when he returned to his father, his father's voice called to him, and the father ran to the son with open arms no matter what he had done. Nothing could ever stop them from being father and son. Where in your life have you recognized the voice of God inviting you, His child, into a more intimate relationship despite your shortcomings?

# 20

# Listening to the Roar Within

My sheep hear My voice, and I know them, and they follow Me. And I give them eternal life, and they shall never
perish; neither shall anyone snatch them out of My hand.

JOHN 10:27–28 NKJV

As I climbed the crude wooden ladder, the bottoms of my
feet felt like they were being hit with ball peen hammers.
The ladder led to a loft ten feet above the floor of a rustic
cabin high in the mountains of Colorado, where I'd been sleeping for the past week. Your body can be totally exhausted from
hiking five to seven miles during a day at almost ten thousand
feet, but the pain from those hardwood rungs can wake you up
like being stung by a hornet.

Within seconds, I was sliding into my bed. It was a heavenly
feeling to slither feet first under the cotton sheets, then cocoon

myself into the wool blankets and fluffy down comforter. As I closed my eyes and settled into the warmth, the pitter patter of a light rain on the roof just above my face was a soothing sound that had me asleep in seconds.

I was rudely awakened by my phone alarm what seemed like only minutes later. It was 4:50 a.m. There comes a time on any expedition when all you want to do is sleep in—the alarm goes off, and your mind screams, *Please, just let me SLEEP!* This was the final morning of the hunt, and to be honest, I was secretly hoping it was raining hard so I'd have an excuse to sleep in. I'm a diehard hunter, fisherman, and outdoorsman—I'm usually the first one up and the last one in after dark—but this morning my body felt like a loaf of bread submerged in peanut butter. Being on alert for potentially life-threatening weather and having to be hyperaware of everything around you while in bear and mountain lion country wears you out, but your life can depend on it. Just five days earlier, I'd had to scramble for cover when I was caught almost a mile from the cabin in a storm that pelted down marble-sized hail. One lightning strike hit so close that if I'd had hair, it would have looked like Albert Einstein's.

I turned off the alarm, stood up, and staggered around while struggling to pull my hooded sweatshirt over my head in the pitch-dark of early morning. (I didn't even know 4:50 *came* twice a day except during hunting season.) However, making my way down that wooden ladder was more effective than shock therapy and coffee in waking me up. By the time I reached the bottom rung, my three hunting buddies were also wide awake from my loud "Ooh!" and "Ow!" with every step.

After downing a cup of instant coffee, I headed to take my turn in the shower. The entire week we were there, the propane tank for the water heater was empty, so we had to shower using water that was not even close to warm. We'd all stand around laughing at the sounds coming from the shower, each guy yelling as if he were being waterboarded on Antarctica.

Then each man headed out to the cold, dark porch to access his sealable storage tub, where each of us stored our camo and base-layer clothing to keep it scent-free. After spraying down with Zero-Odor to eliminate any remaining scent that would alert game animals of our presence or give notice to predators of an easy meal, we'd put on our camo and face paint.

On this particular morning, I had to make a decision. I had both an elk tag and a bear tag. I hadn't had elk come closer than three hundred yards on this trip, but I'd had bear within one hundred yards several times. I had brought along my Remington .30-06 for bear just in case a long-distance shot was all that presented itself, but I'd waited the entire week to take it out. It was a hard choice to make; I'm almost exclusively a bow hunter, and having been on pro staff for Bear Archery for the past twelve years, I felt an obligation to only use bow. As I stood there, something caused me to pause not just for a few seconds but for the better part of a minute. *Do I take my bow or my .30-06?* This uncertainty was *highly* unusual—I almost always take the bow—but something—or Someone—was causing me to rethink my normal "go-to" choice. Finally, I complied with the strong gut instinct that was prompting me to take my rifle. Quickly loading up two full magazines of 150-grain bullets, I slung the Remington steel over my shoulder and slipped into the predawn dark of the Colorado mountains.

I'd walked this trail at least a dozen times during the week-long hunt; I knew every turn and rocky outcropping. I also knew every mud puddle, downed tree, low-hanging limb, and oak scrub bush that, if disturbed, would notify any creature in the vicinity I was intruding into their bedroom and make it a sure bet that I wouldn't see any game animals within range.

## A Voice in the Dark

After approximately three hundred yards, the mountain started going straight uphill, taking me some four hundred feet higher in elevation into another section of timber. I made my way onto a game trail, but I hadn't gone more than a hundred yards when I came to a spot where I always went to the right around a large pine. There was no brush on that side of the tree, making my approach that much stealthier. I was just a few feet away from the pine and about to go to the right when an internal voice stopped me in my tracks. It said, *I want you to go to the left here.* The voice caused me to cock my head like a curious puppy, and then my flesh started having a conversation with my spirit. Yeah, I know—it sounds crazy. And that's exactly what my mind started telling this voice that was trying to get me to go left. I stood there silently arguing that the voice didn't know what it was saying, even questioning if the voice understood how to be a "professional hunter." I heard it a second time. *I know this doesn't make sense to you, but are you willing to be obedient to what I'm asking you to do?* Okay—this was starting to challenge every hunting bone in my body. To go left meant walking through waist-high brush, not only postponing my arrival at my hunting blind (it's crucial to get there before light) but making extra noise, which I had been obsessively careful to avoid.

After standing there for probably thirty seconds having this internal conversation, the voice then asked me a very specific question: *Do you trust Me?* I knew this voice. I'd known it since I was a young boy. It was the same voice that had not only convicted me when I was doing wrong but comforted me in times of trouble. I answered quietly, "Yes, God. I trust You." I took the gun from my shoulder, held it above my head, and made my way left, through the waist-high brush.

Another hundred yards into my hike, I came to another spot where I always go to the right. Again the voice spoke to me and said, *Are you willing to go to the left if I ask you to?* I remember my response: "Really, God?" *Yes.* "Okay, but this doesn't make a whole lot of sense to me because it's *really* delaying me getting set up before first light."

With only three hundred yards left to go, I once again came to a split in the path. To the right was a much easier, less rocky, and brushless trail, but to go to the left meant walking through more brush and moveable rocks than the other two locations combined. I knew what I was about to be asked to do, and I did it without hesitation this time. I didn't understand why, but I'd trusted this voice my whole life, and even if there was no reason for it that I'd ever see or understand in this life, it felt good to hear His voice—the voice of the Holy Spirit—and to be obedient. That He would speak to me so clearly and so intimately made me feel fathered. Loved. He'd asked me three times if I was willing to do something different than I'd done before—something that didn't make sense to me—and my response to my heavenly Father this time was an emphatic *yes*.

First light was now making my steps much easier as I approached the area where I had set up my Primos hunting blind earlier that week. I'd brushed in the blind and tucked it into a little knoll that made it very difficult to see. The only problem with this location was that it had been giving me swirling winds the whole week, meaning I couldn't play the wind to keep from being detected. Inside my blind I had a bottle of Zero-Odor so that I could spray my head and face down to eliminate as much body odor as possible. I also had an elk decoy in the blind that I'd pull out to put other animals at ease, and a collapsible chair to reduce back pain from sitting long hours.

When I reached the area, I was dumbfounded—where was my blind? I could see the brush I'd put all around and on top of it, but no blind. To the right about five yards away was my chair, and in front of the brush pile was the elk decoy and my spray bottle—both riddled with large bite marks. Looking closer, I saw the blind. It was totally flattened. Two words instantly popped into my mind: *rogue bear*. When a bear knows you're there—can hear you, see you, or smell you—and it does something like that, you've got a big problem.

I collected my gear that was strewn about, pulled as much of my blind back together as I could, and crawled in through the back zippered entrance. There, not three feet from the front window, was a still-steaming pile of bear scat. The bear had been there just minutes before. It knew my address.

After making a small opening in the front of the blind, I pulled my gun up beside me, loaded a shell, and picked up my phone to text my buddy, Brandon, about what I'd just discovered. Here was our conversation:

Brent: 6:40 AM

> I got to my blind 10 minutes ago and a bear had flattened it and pulled my stuff out.

Brandon: 6:41 AM

> LOL. He doesn't like you!

Brent: 6:42 AM

> The chair was 5 yards away, and my field spray bottle was chewed up.

**Brandon: 6:44 AM**
He is sending a message. LOL

**Brandon: 6:49 AM**
OK, hear any bugles this morning?

**Brent: 6:49 AM**
Yes, up on Moonshine only.

**Brent: (no time)**
Payback baby . . . dead bear!

**Brent 6:51 AM**
I saw him go down.

**Brandon: (no time)**
You just shot him?

**Brandon: 6:53 AM**
Awesome sauce!

**Brent: 6:53 AM**
Yep. I'm shaking.

**Brent: (no time)**
He was walking right to my blind, back for more.

**Brent: 6:54 AM**
My ears are now plugged.

**Brent: 7:00 AM**
He's dead. I'm standing over him.

Just after texting Brandon at 6:49, I looked out the window opening and there walking straight at me was the rogue bear. It had no fear of me whatsoever. I can't even remember reaching down and grabbing my rifle; everything became as one motion over the next few seconds. As the bear approached, it suddenly turned broadside for a moment to step over a downed tree branch, and that was the last step it ever took. Kaboom! The .30-06 roared and the bear dropped where it stood. From the time I saw it coming toward me until the time it was on the ground was all of five seconds—it happened that fast. Immediately after the shot, my hands, once calm and sure, were shaking uncontrollably. My ears were ringing and plugged from the concussion of the shot in a closed space. I reached for my phone to text Brandon, but I was shaking so badly I kept making mistakes and had to keep undoing my messages because the spelling was so bad.

Had I shown up only minutes earlier, I'd have walked right up on that rogue bear in the process of tearing apart my blind and gear.

After the shaking wore off and I calmed down, I began experiencing a peace that I can't explain; I just felt it—*deeply*. It was the peace that came from the Holy Spirit. There was a reason why the voice kept delaying me on the way to my blind, and in that moment I felt safe—safe in the protection of my Father's care. He *knew*.

Sometimes the instruction of the Holy Spirit will make no sense to your flesh. It may—and often will—go against what your brain is telling you. The question isn't just whether you *trust* His voice. The bigger question is, Do you even *know* His voice?

In the church where I grew up, the Holy Spirit was recognized as a part of the Holy Trinity; He was welcome, but He'd better sit in the back row, keep His hands down, and by all means, keep quiet. That's pretty much how it was in most churches in our area and our denomination when I was a kid. Including the Holy Spirit in a sermon was rare, and when He was included, it was usually more about how the Holy Spirit's role is to convict us of our sin. If that's the only understanding you have of the Holy Spirit, you can quickly come to see Him as the judge, jury, and jailer, rather than being the One who frees you.

## Imputed and Imparted Righteousness

> Oh, the power revealed the first time the lion cub
> roared—
> and understood who he really was.

Throughout this book, we've looked at the different aspects of our roar in almost every chapter. But where does this roar come from? What silences the roar? And what purpose does it serve?

The righteousness of God is not something that can be earned. It is a free gift to those who believe in Christ, have repented of their sins, and receive Christ as Lord and Savior. "Peter said to them, 'Repent, and each of you be baptized in the name of Jesus Christ for the forgiveness of your sins; and you will receive the gift of the Holy Spirit'" (Acts 2:38 NASB). When this happens, God *imputes*, or as Scripture says, "credits to believers," His righteousness (see Rom. 4), enabling Christians to be justified.

Imputed righteousness can be explained this way: God bestows justifying righteousness upon the believer in such a way that it becomes part of his or her person. Because as believers we have the Holy Spirit in us—in our spirits—we have been made totally righteous in God's eyes. And His eyes are the only ones that matter. My spirit (small *s*) is now filled with His Spirit (capital *S*), identifying me as His child and guaranteeing me His promise of eternal life.

> And you also were included in Christ when you heard the message of truth, the gospel of your salvation. When you believed, you were marked in him with a seal, the promised Holy Spirit, who is a deposit guaranteeing our inheritance until the redemption of those who are God's possession—to the praise of his glory. (Eph. 1:13–14)

When a lion is born, it possesses a roar. It is given freely, because that is how God created the lion; it's something that sets it apart from the other animals. When a person is "born again," God gives us a new life. We not only have a new identity as a child of God but, through the Holy Spirit, He imputes to us His righteousness through no deed or merit of our own. That's how He identifies the believer as His child (Eph. 1:13–14). We don't just have a new identity *in Him*, but we now have God *in us*, speaking to us and guiding us.

> But when He, the Spirit of truth, comes, He will guide you into all the truth; for He will not speak on His own initiative, but whatever He hears, He will speak; and He will disclose to you what is to come. (John 16:13 NASB)

The One who is in you, who speaks to you and calls you by name, is the same One who created everything that is!

I was baptized in 1972 at the age of twelve in my home church. I was about fourteen when I first felt like I could hear God's voice speaking to me as I was beginning to mature in my faith. Lying in my bed, I was suddenly overwhelmed by the presence of God and raised both hands toward the ceiling, glorifying God and praising His name. It wasn't something I'd seen anyone do before, because PDA (public display of adoration) was frowned upon in our conservative church. It drove me to my knees, where I thanked God for my life and began a relationship and communication with my heavenly Father that has lasted my whole life.

The next significant time I can recall God clearly speaking to me was the night I was dropped off for my freshman year of college. I'd been working in a steel mill for a couple of years after high school but felt God was leading me to a new place. I sensed a calling, but I didn't yet know what it was, and I prayed for God to open my eyes to what He wanted. As I opened up Scripture, I asked God what He wanted me to hear so that I could know His calling on my life, and the Holy Spirit led me to Psalm 119. As I began reading, this verse popped off the page as if spoken directly to me: "During my brief earthly life I compose songs about your commands" (Ps. 119:54 GNT).

In our part of western Pennsylvania, "real men" didn't sing. That was for women, and if you did sing, you were teased and called a "choir boy" and a lot of other derogatory things. When I arrived at college, my new roommate, Trent, was in the US Navy—and he sang! I had a deep respect for those who served in the military, so when he encouraged me to try out for several vocal ensembles at the college, I listened. I never dreamed I would make it into any of them, but I did. Not only did I make it into choir and male chorus, I was selected into the private voice studio. During my freshman year I was invited to attend NATS (National Association of Teachers of Singing), and to my surprise, I took second place in this national competition. By my sophomore year, I was starting to compose songs and began touring with a guy named Steven Curtis Chapman (before the Curtis part), and we formed the Chapman/Henderson Band. Within two months, the college was sending us all over the United States on tour, and the first song I cowrote with Steven ended up being recorded by the Christian Female Vocalist of the Year, Sandi Patty.

I soon began performing on a much larger platform and writing songs for artists like the New Gaither Vocal Band, Sandi Patty, Ray Boltz, the group ONE, and many others. This happened not only because I *heard* the voice of the Holy Spirit move me to write songs my freshman year but because I *trusted and obeyed* that voice. That gift of God's imparted righteousness enabled me to compose a lot of songs, including four that rose to number one on the Christian Billboard charts, along with another fourteen top-ten hits.

You can hear the voice of the Holy Spirit, but if you don't take time to *know* that voice, you will not trust Him when He speaks and will be vulnerable to listening to any voice. On my own, I never would have chosen singing, songwriting, speaking, or writing books, and I certainly didn't have the ability to do any of it on my own.

God had imputed His righteousness to me, but it was His *imparted* righteousness that enabled me to do what He'd called me to do. Imparted righteousness is what God does in the believer by the power of the Holy Spirit after justification. He works in the Christian to enable and empower the process of sanctification, or becoming more like Christ.

Look at this passage from Romans 4:

If, in fact, Abraham was justified by works, he had something to boast about—but not before God. What does Scripture say? "Abraham believed God, and it was credited to him as righteousness."

Now to the one who works, wages are not credited as a gift but as an obligation. However, to the one who does not work but trusts God who justifies the ungodly, their faith is credited as righteousness. David says the same thing when he speaks of the blessedness of the one to whom God credits righteousness apart from works:

> "Blessed are those
>     whose transgressions are forgiven,
>     whose sins are covered.
> Blessed is the one
>     whose sin the Lord will never count against them."

Is this blessedness only for the circumcised, or also for the uncircumcised? We have been saying that Abraham's faith was credited to him as righteousness. Under what circumstances was it credited? Was it after he was circumcised, or before? It was not after, but before! And he received circumcision as a sign, a seal of the righteousness that he had by faith while he was still uncircumcised. So then, he is the father of all who believe but have not been circumcised, in order that righteousness might be credited to them. (vv. 2–11)

"Faith is credited as righteousness" means God credits, or imputes, His righteousness to the one who has faith. Faith is the abandonment of all claims to be righteous, and, instead, is trusting God who counts the ungodly as righteous.

How do we go on to receive the blessing of God's imparted righteousness? We have to *trust* God and *obey*. God won't ever impose His authority. He will part the sea, but we have to trust Him to lead us to the shore, and we have to get up and walk. That day in the Colorado mountains, the Lion of Judah was speaking directly to me. He put a check in my spirit causing me to pause and listen. His voice was guiding me and keeping me from becoming bear bait, but I had to not only listen to that voice but also *recognize* that the voice was His. I had to trust it with my very life, have a willing spirit, and *act* on it. Once you learn to hear and trust His voice, you will begin to listen to the roar within!

## THE **BIG** QUESTION:

"You can hear the voice of the Holy Spirit, but if you don't take time to *know* that voice, you will not trust Him when He speaks and will be vulnerable to listening to any voice." Where in your life right now are you struggling to hear Him? What's causing the break in the relationship?

# Conquering Our Fear of Darkness

We can easily forgive a child who is afraid of the dark;
the real tragedy of life is when men are afraid of the light.

ROBIN SHARMA

The Alaskan sunset displayed a magnificent array of oranges, reds, blues, and purples as the sun dipped below the horizon, illuminating the flowing water of the Russian River. The dorsal fins of hundreds of silver and pink salmon cut through its surface as they made their way to the falls for one purpose: to spawn so that the next generation would have life, only to give up their own lives shortly thereafter. These fish had journeyed thousands of miles after being in the open seas for three years, called back to the exact place where they were given the gift of life. They were not lost; they were headed on a mission with purpose. It's a journey that's been happening since the beginning of time.

This is one of my favorite spots on earth. It's not a safe place by any stretch of the imagination, but it's fully and dangerously alive, and I love how that awakens my senses. In late summer, it's a hot spot for bald eagles perched over its shallows—easy pickings for an all-you-can-eat fish dinner. As these salmon have made their way from the deep blue waters of the Pacific to Alaska's bountiful streams, they've had to get past incredible obstacles. They've avoided being snagged in the gill nets of thousands of commercial fishing boats. They've eluded pods of killer whales, eagles, harbor seals, seal nets, and fishermen. And finally, they've had to escape the one animal that keeps me looking over my shoulder like no other on the planet, the Alaskan brown bear. Wherever you find streams choked with huge salmon, you will find these massive carnivores. The waters of the Russian River are both beautiful and deadly. The river has teeth, and if you stand in one place too long and don't watch your back, you may find yourself on the menu. The flip side of that is if you pay too much attention, always looking over your shoulder, it's easy to get turned around. If that happens, things can get dangerous real fast. Before you know it, the sun is going down, wolves begin to howl, and the rogue bears you don't see in daylight are now silently walking the well-worn paths along the banks of the river. Those who have made this mistake soon find themselves desperately searching for the last rays of sun to illuminate their path out of this shadowy maze of terror. It's a toxic fear that quickly spreads like a viper's venom and sinks its fangs deep into your core.

It was the last day of August. Daylight was getting shorter as the chill of fall moved in, and a friend and I were filming bears on the banks of the Russian River. This time of year, many of the salmon had already given up their lives after spawning, and their rotting remains were washed up all along the shoreline, filling the air with the odor of death and decay. That smell keeps many tourists and fishermen away, but it's like a dinner bell for brown bears from miles around.

## Alaskan Darkness

When we arrived at our shoot location, we had another man with us who hadn't come to film. He was a relative of the man I was with and was only there to fish before the season came to an end. We had just a few hours of daylight left, so we agreed not to put too much distance between him and us so that when it was time to leave, we could walk the path back up the steep embankment together. His job was to pay attention to where we were and not get out of visual contact.

After several hours, this plan fell apart. He was so busy concentrating on the fish and we were so focused on capturing video that we wandered apart. Realizing that the sun's final rays were about to disappear, we started looking for our lost friend. Things can go south quickly in this environment once the sun goes down; we began shouting his name, but the sound of the moving water and the distance between us were too much. We waited as long as we could in the darkness before we finally had to call it. Knowing this man had lived in Alaska for years and understood what can happen when the lights go out, we made the decision to make our way up the steep hill and back to the truck without him.

When we arrived back at the parking area, there were no other vehicles or people in sight. Our stomachs quickly jumped into our throats. Alaska is beautiful and brutal and will eat you for lunch if you're not paying attention—and someone definitely hadn't been paying attention.

After waiting at the truck for about thirty minutes, thinking maybe he'd simply misjudged how far he'd walked down the river and would show up any minute, we outlined our options. In the lower 48 we have all kinds of fallback plans; we have a plan A, a plan B, a plan C, and finally a plan D if disaster happens. Plan D is always a last resort when all else has failed; it's like cutting away your main parachute when it doesn't open and hoping that the reserve chute deploys. Each plan has different levels of action. In Alaska, there usually isn't time for plans B and C, as situations can become deadly dangerous in no time flat. Since plan A didn't pan out, and with rogue bears now making their way through the darkness toward the smell of rotting fish, it was time to execute plan D: search and rescue.

Sometimes there's no time to go get help or wait for help to arrive. There are moments when time is critical, and this was one of those times. My friend holstered his 9-millimeter, grabbed a flashlight, and began the journey into the black night. Honestly, a 9-millimeter isn't really going to do much to a massive brown bear unless you have the gun in its mouth when you pull the trigger; something more along the lines of a .500 Magnum is about the only handgun that's going to do that job. (The .500 Magnum is among the most powerful revolvers in the world since its original release and has been touted as the world's most powerful handgun.)

After about another half hour of waiting, each second feeling like a full minute as I stood there alone, dreading having to go into the darkness if they didn't show up shortly, I traded my bear pepper spray for my .44 Mag, grabbed my flashlight, and walked to the top of the hill, scanning the darkness. It was as black as if I'd put on a sleep mask—not a glimmer of light.

I knew I had to walk into the biggest fear I'd ever faced in the wilds; I thought, *I can't believe I'm doing this!* But there were now *two* men in harm's way. Despite the fear telling me that I could become the third, I began walking down the hill and into my fears. On the inside, I silently recited Psalm 23:4, *Even though I walk through the valley of the shadow of death, I will fear no evil, for You are with me; Your rod and Your staff, they comfort me.* On the outside, I was walking with a flashlight in one hand and my Taurus Raging Bull in the other, saying loudly, "Hey, bear! Hey, bear!" One thing you don't want to do is spook a brown bear. (On the other hand, you don't want to be a walking dinner bell either . . .)

When I arrived at the bear path that ran along the riverbank, I had no idea which direction my friend had gone. I assumed he'd gone to the right, as that was the last position we could remember seeing our missing fisherman. Believing he had that direction covered, I turned left. Within about two hundred yards, my light illuminated several tiny reflections on the ground not ten feet in front of me. When I directed the beam of the flashlight there, I saw, scattered in a three-foot circle, pink plastic steelhead worms, roe, and silver spoons used for catching silver salmon. I knew no one would have left the contents of their tackle box lying on the ground like that unless they'd been knocked down. Instantly my stomach was in my throat. If he'd been hammered, I knew his body wouldn't be far away; bears will drag their kill a short distance, cover it with brush after they feed, and not stray far from their pile. Instantly, I felt the hairs on the back of my neck stand up as if a lightning strike were about to happen. If there was a body with a killer bear close by, this was like being in chum-filled waters. It's hard to make heads or tails of your thoughts when you know that a bear's breath could smell like you in a matter of seconds. I desperately needed wisdom to prevail, but my mind was racing even faster than my heart. I quickly made a scan of the area and headed straight back up the hill to the truck for help. I desperately wanted to run, but I knew better—running with my back turned from a carnivore would trigger its predator instinct.

When I crowned the top of the steep hill, I could see the welcome sight of not one but two flashlights coming toward me. It was my friend and the fisherman I was afraid had become a bear pile. He'd gotten lost and ended up about a half mile downstream from his planned exit. My relief was great—partly because he was alive, and partly because I was no longer alone in the dark with creatures higher than me on the food chain.

We never did figure out why the contents of a tackle box were left scattered on the trail.

## Running toward Our Fears

There are many times in our lives when a situation, at first glance, seems dire, scary—even impossible. Fear urges us to retreat to our safe place, the place where we think we can remove ourselves from hurt, shame, or risk. Sometimes the opposite is true, and we charge blindly into a situation without all the information, tools, or weapons we need, causing even more damage. We already possess the ultimate weapon that can stop the enemy's lies in their tracks, but when he spews his filthy, foul breath on us, we forget who we really are. We're afraid we're next on the menu, and our fight-or-flight response takes over. Whether fear causes us to charge blindly into a situation or to disengage and flee, either response develops a pattern of self-protection. We become self-reliant, not trusting God. Charging toward *or* running from our fears without God's guidance and wisdom is a trust issue—always.

How do we run toward the roar instead of away from it? How do we build that depth of trust and love that casts out all fear? One of my greatest fears as I've been getting older is facing the future, not knowing how many more years I will be able to go on amazing adventures, travel the world, and disciple other men. Will I get cancer, have a heart attack, get hit by a car, suffer a massive stroke, or experience all four like my father did? Fearing the future—facing the unknown—is like walking into the darkness. Those are the rogue bears in my brain that keep me up at night, and every one of those thoughts is rooted in either the past or the future.

Healthy fear and healthy anger will drive us to do the right thing. But unhealthy fear and unhealthy anger can turn into a pretend masculinity that prevents us from living out the life God has planned for us. What is the reason behind unhealthy fear and anger? The common denominator is a lack of trust in God.

Unhealthy fear and unhealthy anger are trust issues. They happen when

1. we don't trust that God is who He says He is.
2. we don't trust that we are who God says we are.

Over the past year, I was invited to be part of a cohort of nationwide Christian speakers and leaders through Trueface, an organization that mentors communicators with God's message of grace and love for the purpose of discipling others. During our first two communicators' cohorts, we were all asked to share our stories, the hidden-card-in-the-deck stories where truth is exposed and masks taken off. Each of us wanted to hide in a closet when asked to share honestly (and sometimes painfully), but we also wanted to run to "get it all out there." It is amazing when we are totally honest about our lives and find that sharing our stories actually endears us to others rather than driving them away. It's powerful when men come alongside each other, saying, "I'm with you, brother," and we are no longer held back by the opinions of others but instead are supported in our struggles.

In our cohort, we processed the limitations of trying to live life without trust. Below is the list that Trueface created to help us understand how important trusting God is.

Without trust:

- I cannot meet God.
- I cannot please God.
- I cannot experience truth and freedom. The truth will not set me free unless I trust it.
- I cannot experience love. If I don't trust you, I can't experience your love, no matter how much love you have for me.
- I cannot live in humility. Humility is trusting God and others with me.
- I cannot develop character. Character is formed as I trust truth and act upon it. Truth only transforms when it is trusted.

- I live in isolation. I am hidden, my character is immature, and I am vulnerable to my weaknesses.
- Truth is relative. I live as my own expert.
- I will live with fear. The perfect love of God (and others) will not cast out fear unless I trust that love.
- Pleasure is substituted for intimacy.
- Power is pursued; the weak are ignored.
- Rights are demanded as the presumed basis for fulfillment.
- I compromise or lose my identity.
- The unhealthy (shame-based) story I tell myself feeds my emotional and relational sickness.
- I lose hope.
- I lose my identity.
- My unhealthy self-story feeds my dysfunctions.
- I am trapped in a mind-set of "I ought to . . ."
- I can reach my potential, but never experience my destiny.[1]

When we can't, don't, or won't trust, we will walk in fear. That raises the question, How do we learn to trust? In order for us to trust God, we need to understand who God is. Our present culture doesn't even know what that means; we have become narcissistic, drowning in entitlement, fame, and self-centeredness. Dysfunction is something we no longer work on correcting; instead, we make reality TV shows out of it, drawing millions to tune in to glorify incredibly dysfunctional behavior—making stars out of black holes.

Can you imagine what would happen if, instead of glorifying and promoting poor behavior, we actually had shows that broke down the lies these reality actors are buying into, helped them untangle what's causing the unhealthy behaviors, and walked them back to health? Such a show would probably be cancelled, because people want to see others who are more screwed up than they are so they can feel good about themselves.

We have lost our way. We do not trust because we've come to believe that truth is relative, that there is no "true north." When there is no true north on a compass, you can never find your way home. You will be guided by the way the wind is blowing or by taking the easiest path.

In today's world, there are many parents who don't want their children to have fewer material possessions than their classmates have. My ten-year-old stepdaughter is always asking for a cell phone—she says all the kids in her class have them and carry them at school. My sixteen-year-old stepdaughter talks about how the other kids in her class are given cars from their parents—not ten-year-old used cars, but BMWs, Mustangs, and other high-end rides. When we keep our children from experiencing any kind of pain or from working hard to save their own money to buy what they want so they understand the value of those things, we cripple them. We bail them out of difficult circumstances so that they can be the popular student and we can become the popular parent. I have coached many parents who say, "I want my child to trust me, to be my friend, to never go without what I didn't have, to know how much I love them, and that I would do anything for them!" Yeah. You're helping them, all right—helping them to fail. You're taking a baseball bat to their knees, keeping them from learning how to walk through tough stuff themselves.

Years ago I wrote a song called "Have We Taught Our Children Well?"

> Have we taught our children well?
> Is our life a show and tell?
> Can they see the love of Jesus in our eyes?
> When another page has turned,
> Do you think that they will have learned
> To show the love of Jesus in their lives?
> Have we taught our children well?

We must be willing to work on our own sin and dysfunction, openly share with our children about our personal shipwrecks, and teach and constantly remind them of their true identity *in Christ* and how untangling the enemy's lies with God's truth transforms us and sets us free (Rom. 12:2). Unless we do that, trusting Christ for them will be like trying to keep their heads above water during a hurricane with a weight tied around their neck. We will not have thrown them a life ring, and we will not have taught them to swim—we'll have taught them how to drown in self-sufficiency and pride because of a lack of trust.

Men view trust as weakness. *Why would I need to trust someone?* We see trusting and depending on another as "I'm not enough." We need to help others understand the amazing, absolute *goodness* of God. Renewing our minds is vital in learning to trust God. If your theology doesn't touch your reality, you haven't experienced the power and love of God's grace.

There are going to be times when we are called to walk dangerous shores with an enemy who is tracking us and wants us to focus on the muddy path and see the impression of his dagger-like claws. He wants to get so close that we can smell the stench of his foul, lying breath and feel the heat of it on our necks. He wants us to feel his bared canines scoring our scalps as he tries to swallow us whole. He wants us to be so afraid that we run and hide or try to overcome him with the self-confidence that comes from our weak mortal flesh. He wants us to fear death itself.

But the enemy doesn't get to call the shots! Matthew 28:18 says, "Jesus came to them and said, 'All authority in heaven and on earth has been given to me.'" What exactly does *all* mean? Is there any authority that Jesus does not have? No! He is trustworthy! It makes *total sense* to trust Him—*we were created to do so*.

Trusting God is a choice, but it is the power of the Holy Spirit that gives us the ability to trust. The more I learn to listen to His voice, the more I learn to trust God and the less I sin. As the old hymn says, "My hope is built on nothing less than Jesus's blood and righteousness."[2] When we understand that **Christ in us is our true identity**, who or what is there left to fear? The more we choose to renew our minds with God's truth, the more the Holy Spirit transforms our thoughts and demolishes our unhealthy emotions, and our fear of the darkness is conquered by the light. We are counted as warriors.

> The LORD is my light and my salvation—
>     whom shall I fear?
> The LORD is the stronghold of my life—
>     of whom shall I be afraid? (Ps. 27:1)

## THE **BIG** QUESTION:

Men, we know God has called us to go and make disciples, but because most of us have never been taught how, we're afraid to try. Can you identify what you are afraid of? If you really trusted that God is who He says He is and that you are who He says you are—and that He will never take you someplace without going before you— would you be willing to follow? What might that next step look like for you?

# The Final Adventure

## ADVENTURE BEGINS
## WHEN YOUR PLANS GO BAD

I n September 2019, I was headed back to Colorado to hunt with three of my buddies. It had been only twelve months since I'd dumped the rogue bear who had torn my blind apart and headed back to take a bite out of me. Scenarios like that have a way of burning deep into your psyche. Those are the moments when everything you've been taught comes to the surface, and what you really believe is forced into the open. In certain circumstances, you get only one shot at making the right decision.

If you've ever heard me speak or read any of my books, you've heard me talk about my friend Wade. He was mentored by an Athabaskan Indian who taught him not only how to survive the most perilous predicaments the wilds can dish out but also about a relationship with Jesus Christ. Wade was not just an armchair storyteller bragging with his "one time" survivor stories—he was a real "man's man" who had lived through more life-and-death situations than a hundred other men combined. His real-life, edge-of-your-seat stories captivated me and drew me into a life of adventure that few get to experience. I have been blessed to be on many adventures with him, and even more blessed to call him friend. We had a saying: "Adventure begins when your plans go bad!"

One of my most vivid memories is a call from Wade after he had just experienced one of those adventures. While he was filming moose in Alaska, the small plywood shack he'd been staying in had been ripped apart by a ten-foot-tall, twelve-hundred-pound brown bear with attitude. He said it looked like it had snowed around the cabin—the bear had pulled out and shredded the pillows and sleeping bags between him and what he was after. The hunter who'd been in the cabin the day before had taken a moose, and there had still been bags of bloody meat lying on the cabin floor that couldn't be flown out until the pilot came back several days later. The only thing Wade had to cover the massive hole the bear had torn in the side of the cabin was a plastic tarp—no match for the muscle, canines, and four-inch claws of a brown bear.

The most intense part of the story was when he and his guide had to spend another night in the shack before they could be flown out. It would be a sleepless night; they knew the bear would return to try to claim what it didn't get the first time. Wade and his guide had high-powered rifles, but it was how Wade renewed his mind that night that kept his thoughts straight in the dark as the bear circled their cabin for several hours, sometimes standing and scoring the tin roof with its enormous claws.

I've shared already how important Derek was to me as a guide in the spiritual wilderness. He mentored me almost daily for about a decade, teaching me how to untangle the lies causing anxiety, shame, worry, fear, and doubt. Wade had been a guide to me through the physical wilderness, and in return I'd been blessed to help guide him through the spiritual wilderness by teaching him how to renew his mind. Those two things were the perfect mix for what Wade faced that night. As he told me the story, he shared that renewing his mind became his most important weapon. If our thoughts go south in a bad situation, our emotions and actions will follow. He had to keep his head on straight. Remember, beliefs shape the thoughts that drive our emotions and actions—this was definitely a test of what Wade *really* believed.

As it turns out, one of the passages he and I had gone over before he'd left for this trip was James 1:2–8.

Consider it a sheer gift, friends, when tests and challenges come at you from all sides. You know that under pressure, your faith-life is forced into the open and shows its true colors. So don't try to get out of anything prematurely. Let it do its work so you become mature and well-developed, not deficient in any way.

If you don't know what you're doing, pray to the Father. He loves to help. You'll get his help, and won't be condescended

to when you ask for it. Ask boldly, believingly, without a second thought. People who "worry their prayers" are like wind-
whipped waves. Don't think you're going to get anything from
the Master that way, adrift at sea, keeping all your options open.
(MSG)

This was one of those "adventure begins when your plans
go bad" moments, and what Wade truly believed was about
to come to the surface. Wade told me what happened next:
"Before crawling in my sleeping bag, I decided to see if there
was a lock on the cabin door (as if the bear would care). As I
stepped across the meat to the door, I saw two eight-penny
nails and a shoestring—that was the lock. Heading back to my
sleeping bag, I said [to my guide], 'Wait! I have an idea! Lie
down in your bunk and put your flashlight on that old bucket
next to your shoulder, then lean your rifle against the bucket
and position it so you can pick it up and point it fast. I'll lay
my gun on this pile of meat and set my flashlight right on top
here. Now lie down and close your eyes. When I say go, with our
eyes still closed, we reach for our flashlights and grab our rifles
and point at the wall. Ready? Go!' We figured if the bear came
back during the night, he'd surely come in through the tarp, so
we'd turn on our flashlights, grab our rifles, and shoot him in
the face. That was our plan. At least it gave us some comfort.

"After practicing our plan several times, and after some nervous
laughter, the knob on the lantern was turned off and darkness
closed in. Brent, at this point all I could think about—besides

this colossal carnivore wanting his dinner which was lying right next to me—was you telling me to be on the lookout for a situation that causes me to have unhealthy thoughts, emotions, and actions. Well, I think this met your criteria. So I started to pray. 'Hello, God—Wade here out in bear country again. Do You remember our plan? It goes like this: Thanks for making these giant carnivores. I will be busy all day keeping an eye on 'em in the daylight. In review: It's Your job to keep an eye on them at night. It's night now, so it's Your turn. Good night.' Then I handed it all over to God. It worked like a dream—I was asleep in five minutes.

"I'm not sure just what time it was when it all happened—must have been around 2:00 or 3:00 a.m. I was sound asleep when the entire cabin began to shake. At first just little quivers, then it really shook and was noisy. Both of us were awake in a flash. We each took a breath and then out of the darkness just below my feet I heard my friend say, 'Wade, tell me that was you.' Without any hesitation I said, 'Grab your gun!' We both snatched our lights and turned them on, shouldered rifles and pointed them at the raking claws on the wall above the table, an arm's-reach away.

"Then the most amazing thing happened with absolutely no premeditation. We both dropped into 'plan A'—we screamed like little girls! Boy, did we make a racket! I have never before or since made that much noise. We shouted nonstop for about two solid minutes while pointing our rifles at the wall until my buddy raised his hand. We both stopped as if a switch had been flipped. We stared at the wall. Maybe five minutes passed as we sat wide-eyed, rifles ready, marinating in adrenaline. We were still sitting on our bunks, still in our sleeping bags, flashlights trained on the flimsy plywood.

"We began to breathe normally after about ten minutes. Just when we were ready to stretch out, it happened again. We could hear his claws on the roof, and his chest pushed against the heaving wall. We could hear his belly hair rubbing on the half-inch plywood that had been getting weaker since Eisenhower was president. This was a rogue bear—the kind of bear that mauls and kills people.

"We made eye contact, and immediately voiced our plan B: 'When his head comes through the wall, we both shoot him in the face.' We aimed at the wall for another minute without breathing, and then my friend motioned me to shift my aim to the left. He stood up and reached across the table, then pounded his hand against the wall at the bear's face level. He then sat down quickly, and we both aimed at the spot where we'd heard the bear breathing.

"I really don't know what happened next, because neither of us was interested in going outside to check. Sometime between the hand-pounding and the half-an-hour-later mark, the bear left. We waited another twenty minutes or so and then checked it off as finished—turned off our light and lay back down. Brent, before drifting off to sleep, I realized that I needed to renew my mind again with God's truth. I thought about Paul's words in Philippians 1:21, 'For to me, to live is Christ, and to die is gain.' And then I focused on another truth. 'If anything happens to me tonight, the first face I'm going to see when I awake is Jesus.' After renewing my mind with those two things, I actually slept really well the rest of the night!" Wade finished.

How can it be that in the middle of a life-and-death circumstance, we can actually find peace and rest? Because that's what the Word of God does. It cuts fear and worry out of our souls and replaces them with courage and absolute assurance. We no longer have to worry about life and death; if things go south, I know I'm headed north, because to live is Christ, and to die is gain!

The following day, the two men were flown back to safety. What happened to the rogue bear that was terrorizing the night? Wade told me, "A week later, a bowhunter and his guide arrived at that camp—the cabin looked like a bomb had exploded. There was no way they could stay there, so they got two spike camp tents. The two-tent idea is that you cook, hang out, and store food and gear in one tent, and sleep ten feet away in the other. It's a great plan in brown bear country.

"It almost always takes multiple shots to take down one of these giants. Picture this: this hunter has never seen a wild brown bear in his life. The first night in bear country, the guide and the bowhunter are asleep in one tent, in sleeping bags in their tighty-whities. About midnight, they are awakened by the sound of nylon ripping and stoves and gear crashing. Ten feet away the gear tent is being assaulted. The guide whispers to the hunter, 'I think we may have a bear out there. I need you to unzip the tent, then dash out and shine your light on the

bear. I'll be right behind you with my rifle. Don't be scared—
I may need to shoot a warning shot to chase the bear away.
Okay—GO!'

"The brave hunter—in his skivvies—unzips the tent in one
big motion and jumps out into the night armed with a flashlight. He shines the beam on the other tent and sees that it's
crushed and collapsed—and there's a Volkswagen-sized brown
bear standing on it. The guide is right behind him with a bolt-
action .338 Winchester Magnum with a 3 x 9 power scope.

"Before the guide can even shoulder the rifle, the bear woofs,
lays down his ears, and charges. The guide raises the gun to waist
level and fires. Fire leaps out of the barrel and reaches halfway
to the bear. The bullet, guided by God, hits the bear just above
the right eye and drops him in a pile only three steps away. The
hunter with the flashlight is rapidly exiting the scene. But it is
pitch-dark and the guide isn't sure what has happened.

"The guide, fully appreciating the mortal danger of the moment, and not knowing if he even hit the bear on the first shot,
rapidly ejects the first shell, works the bolt, aims at the bear,
and 'click' . . . no bang. He runs the bolt again . . . 'click.' Shouting for the light, he looks down at his feet; in its beam he sees
three shells in the grass by his bare toes. The floor plate of his
rifle is swinging open; it had opened on the recoil of the first
shot and dropped all the shells into the grass. But the bear is
dead as a doornail—and it's definitely the rogue bear that had
assaulted our cabin. Like we always say, 'Adventure begins when
your plans go bad!'"

What strikes me in this story is that the guide ended up only having one shot, but that was all it took. There's an old hymn we used to sing in church, "A Mighty Fortress Is Our God," and one line from it especially stands out to me: "One little word shall fell him."[1] When the guide, who was trained to use his weapon, let loose with the roar of the .338, he only needed one shot to dispose of that bear. In the same way, when we understand who we are in Christ, listen to the voice of the Holy Spirit, and know and trust the power of God's Word, the roar that comes from His truth will drop the enemy in his tracks.

## Back to Colorado

I know the intensity of being charged by a big-game animal—it's happened to me on several occasions. You have until the count of one to make the right decision, or things aren't going to turn out well. Having had large animals charge me in the past helped my actions on this trip back to Colorado.

I'd been bow hunting since the early morning hours with my attention focused on taking an elk. As darkness approached, I noticed a large dark shadow at about eighty yards. I knew it wasn't an elk—it was too low to the ground—and it was moving like a tank in my direction. Bear.

I'd already marked the distance to an opening in front of me as being thirty-two yards. As the bear approached this open shooting lane, I came to full draw. It was instinctive—I've been in this position many times. As I prepared for the shot, bow-string anchored against my cheek, the bear stepped into the opening. Once I knew it was where I needed it to stop, I let out a loud "meh" sound to freeze it in its tracks. The second it froze, my arrow was already on its way to what I knew would be a fatal shot. What I didn't expect was that as soon as the arrow found its mark, the bear made a full-on charge straight at me. As it covered the distance faster than I thought possible, its teeth were bared and it was snarling—it was on a search-and-destroy mission. The bear would be on me in a matter of two seconds; my instincts took over. The camouflage I was wearing that day was a leafy camo, meaning there were leaves sewn onto the fabric to make me look like a small tree or bush. The leaves moved with the wind, blending me in with my surroundings. As the bear approached at high speed, I didn't move—not one inch. I let my camo do its work. I trusted it, and it potentially saved my life. The bear passed within three feet of me and never knew I was there. It all happened so fast there was no time to think or even wet my pants. Standing still and letting my cover work for me was instinctive. I'd been here before, and trusting what I was wearing helped me make the right choice.

There are those moments when our faith-life is forced into the open, and we have to trust that the One who made us truly knows us and will give us what we need when we need it. In that instant, there was no time to renew my mind; things happened way too fast. But having renewed my mind for years with God's promises and having had an intimate relationship with Him my whole life took the fear and the what-ifs out of my thought patterns because I've come to love and trust Him. Being able to walk without fear is one of the greatest gifts God has ever given us. That can only happen when we understand that our true identity is in Christ. *That* is the source from which our roar comes.

◀◀◀◀⟨⟩▶▶

What I'm about to share is one of the most difficult things I've ever had to experience. It is part of a chapter I knew I'd have to write someday, but it came much too quickly.

There is a time when this life's adventures come to a close and the next great adventure begins, a time when death stalks us like a thief in the night, sometimes without warning, but we have nothing to fear. God has planned for this life's adventures to end so that the greatest adventure of all—our *real* life—can begin.

If you've ever gotten a call or text in the middle of the night, you've felt that instant knot in your stomach that says, *Something's wrong*. I've had far too many of those over the past few years. In less than four years I grieved the loss of both parents, a twenty-eight-year marriage, two cousins, an aunt, three uncles, a prayer partner, and five of my closest friends. When you believe you've cried all the tears you have and think you can no longer feel pain, something will make you aware that deep, soul-level grief and pain still exist; it's a shock to the heart that reminds you that this isn't heaven yet.

I was awakened around 4:30 a.m. one day with something stirring my spirit. I wasn't hungry, and I didn't need to use the bathroom. There was a feeling of grief deep in my core for a reason yet unknown. Because of the huge amount of loss I've experienced in recent years, I won't look at my phone in the middle of the night; I turn the sounds and vibrate mode off at bedtime. There comes a time when your mind and body can no longer deal with the possibility of getting bad news in the middle of the night. It'll keep you from sleeping, which will wear you down, causing unhealthy thoughts and emotions. But there is an inner voice that will speak to you right when you need it, even awaken you from slumber—a gentle voice that is always right on time. It's the voice of the Shepherd, and His sheep hear His voice. The voice of the Holy Spirit prompted me to check my phone that early morning, and I discovered that the man with whom I'd shared a ministry and traveled the world was dying. Wade was on the last page of his final chapter.

Brotherhood goes beyond normal friendship. Only those who have faced life-and-death situations together and had to rely upon each other to survive can ever truly understand that—and we'd had our share of near-death experiences together. We'd shared countless campfires together, listened to roaring lions under an African night sky, been close enough to Alaskan brown bears to smell their breath, and even experienced shipwrecks, both on the sea and in our personal lives. In the end it wouldn't be a shipwreck that would take his life, or even the cancer he'd battled for almost a decade. Only God could take his life, and that would only happen when God said it was time.

In Wade's final hours, I received a call from a mutual brother in Christ, Tabb, who was able to pray with him. Even in his bedridden state, unable to talk, Wade was still able to wink at Tabb, letting him know that death would never keep him from real life—eternal life. This once larger-than-life man's man was no longer able to physically fight the good fight, but make no mistake—like that one bullet that killed the bear, his one silent wink roared the never-ending truth of the gospel in Philippians 1:21, "For to me, to live is Christ and to die is gain!"

Wade and I would always share with men, "When a man knows who he is in Christ, that he is created in the image of the living God, and is no longer held captive by the opinions of others or cares whether he lives or dies, that man is now extremely dangerous—dangerous for *good*!" That is the power that comes when you unleash your one, true identity in Christ.

"Adventure begins when your plans go bad!" My friend and brother is now on the greatest adventure of his life—one that will never end. Godspeed, Wade Nolan. I'll see you in the next great adventure.

We have been on a journey together through this book. We've journeyed from the cradle to the grave, to the brink of death and back. We've exposed the lies of the enemy, and we've discovered how to take him out. But now this is about *your* story, about becoming the man God created you to be before the very foundations of the earth. What is your story? Who are you really? What has held you back? Do you trust your heavenly Father? Do you believe that you are who He says you are? Now that you have the tools, are you ready to risk doing something different with your life—ready to seek out, accept, and move forward into the purpose for which God created you?

It's time to go change the lives of as many men as you can, because *changed men change men!* "The LORD is a warrior; the LORD is His name" (Exod. 15:3 NASB). It's time to become the warrior God designed you to be. It's time to unleash the powerful truth of who you really are. You have what it takes, for you possess THE ROAR WITHIN!

# Acknowledgments

Chip—thank you for believing in me and choosing me to be a part of your writer's quiver. Your wisdom, insights, guidance, and friendship have been vitally important to completing this project so that this message can transform lives all around the world.

Rachel—from the very start you wanted to make this book not just good but great! You have pushed me beyond what my eyes could see and given your time, insights, and passion to see the lives of men transformed. Thank you for investing your heart in this message.

Sandi—you are simply amazing! All those books you read as a kid while your sister and I were outside building forts and getting into trouble at Grandma's house have served you well. You are the other side of my brain. You know just what I am thinking and trying to say—you just say it much better (and with fewer words)! This book would *not* be what it is today without your countless hours of editing, suggestions, and loving me well by helping me move from storyteller to author. You rock!

Stacy—babe, just thinking of you puts a smile on my face. I can't even put into words how much I love you. Your story is one of beauty from ashes. You are tender and caring, yet strong and courageous when you need to be. You breathed life into this man who was doing little more than surviving; your inner and outer beauty awaken my soul. At 4:30 a.m., you quietly get up and go to work every single day. You don't do it for applause, accolades, or social media likes—you do it out of love. You are an amazing mother, a frontline healthcare worker, an awesome decorator, my helper, my love, and my best friend. Your sacrifices have helped me stay true to my calling and helped change the lives of thousands of men. I am so blessed to call you my wife.

My Lord and Savior, Jesus Christ—everything belongs to and comes from You. I worship You for who You are, and I'm humbled that You'd make Your home in me. Your grace changed everything in my life when I was at the very bottom. You've allowed me to proclaim Your name, the name which is above ALL names. You're faithful to the promises that You've called me to—without fail. You know my darkest thoughts, yet You're pleased to call me Your child. I am a child of the one true King, and no one and nothing can ever take that away from me. I am so grateful to call You Father, and I'm so proud to be Your son. Thank You for forgiving my sins—all of them—and for keeping no record of my wrongs. Here I am, Lord—send me.

# Notes

### Chapter 1  The Big Question

1. John Eldredge, *Wild at Heart* (Nashville: Thomas Nelson, 2001), 114.

2. Eldredge, *Wild at Heart*, 9.

3. *Braveheart*, directed by Mel Gibson (1995; Hollywood, CA: Paramount Home Video, 2002), DVD.

### Chapter 3  The Big Five Man-Killers #1

1. *First Blood*, directed by Ted Kotcheff (1982; Santa Monica, CA: Artisan Entertainment, 1998), DVD.

2. *Braveheart*.

### Chapter 4  Finding Your Swing

1. *The Legend of Bagger Vance*, directed by Robert Redford (Los Angeles: 20th Century Fox, 2000), DVD.

2. *Legend of Bagger Vance*.

3. *Legend of Bagger Vance*.

4. *Legend of Bagger Vance*.

### Chapter 5  When Brave Men Stand

1. Billy Graham, "A Time for Moral Courage," *Reader's Digest*, July 1964.

2. Nelson Mandela, *Long Walk to Freedom* (New York: Little, Brown, 1994), 622.

### Chapter 6 Come to the Waters

1. *The Lion King*, directed by Roger Allers and Rob Minkoff (1994; Burbank, CA: Walt Disney Pictures, 2003), DVD.

2. *Lion King*.

### Chapter 7 The Big Five Man-Killers #2

1. Ben Sisario, "How Aretha Franklin's 'Respect' Became a Battle Cry for Musicians Seeking Royalties," *New York Times*, August 17, 2018, https://www.nytimes.com/2018/08/17/arts/aretha-franklin-respect-copyright.html.

### Chapter 8 From Bald Spots to Blind Spots

1. *Gladiator*, directed by Ridley Scott (Los Angeles: Dreamworks Home Entertainment, 2000), DVD.

### Chapter 10 The Big Five Man-Killers #3

1. "Unusual African Buffalo Facts: Why Are They So Feared by Hunters?" African Wildlife Detective, accessed August 12, 2020, https://www.africa-wildlife-detective.com/african-buffalo.html.

### Chapter 12 Quieting the Angry Roar

1. "Why Porn Leaves Consumers Lonely," Fight the New Drug, August 23, 2017, https://fightthenewdrug.org/why-porn-leaves-consumers-lonely/.

### Chapter 18 Counted as Warriors

1. *Braveheart*.

2. Timothy Keller, as quoted in *The Heart of Man Participant's Guide* (The Heart of Man, 2017), 42.

3. Keller, as quoted in *Heart of Man Participant's Guide*, 5.

4. *Tombstone*, directed by George P. Cosmatos (1993; Hollywood, CA: Hollywood Pictures Home Entertainment, 2010), DVD.

5. Timothy Keller, Twitter post by @timkellernyc, 11:05 a.m., February 23, 2015, https://twitter.com/timkellernyc/status/569890726349307904?lang=en.

## Chapter 19  Recognizing the Roar Within

1. Henry T. Blackaby and Richard Blackaby, *Hearing God's Voice* (Nashville: B&H, 2002), 143.

2. Jonathan Edwards, "A Divine and Supernatural Light," in *The Sermons of Jonathan Edwards: A Reader* (Yale, 1999), 127–28.

## Chapter 21  Conquering Our Fear of Darkness

1. This list used by permission of Trueface, www.Trueface.org.

2. "My Hope Is Built on Nothing Less," Edward Mote (1834).

## Chapter 22  The Final Adventure

1. "A Mighty Fortress Is Our God *(Ein feste Burg ist unser Gott)*," Martin Luther (c. 1531).

# About the Author

**Brent Alan Henderson** is an in-demand speaker, author, professional outdoorsman, John Maxwell certified life coach, ordained pastor, and recording artist. He's toured with Dove and Grammy Award–winning artists including Steven Curtis Chapman, Sandi Patty, Avalon, and Crystal Lewis. Brent has been featured at hundreds of outreach events, including the Billy Graham Crusade and Promise Keepers. He also speaks more than fifty times a year at men's retreats, wild game dinners, men's conferences, schools, and churches all around the world. Brent understands what makes men tick, how to capture their attention, and how to move men to action. His transformational message has moved over thirteen thousand men to receive Christ in just the past decade. Brent's hard-to-top guy stories and powerful message will guide you through the wilderness, equip you to *crush* the lies of the evil one, and awaken the roar within.

# Get to know
# **BRENT!**

Learn more about Brent at
**menministry.org**

To book him to speak at your next event, head to
**mitchellgroup.org**

---

🐦 @BrentAHenderson    📘 Brent Henderson    📷 BrentAHenderson

LET'S
TALK
ABOUT
BOOKS

- Share or mention the book on your social media platforms. Use the hashtag **#TheRoarWithin**.

- Write a book review on your blog or on a retailer site.

- Pick up a copy for friends, family, or anyone who you think would enjoy and be challenged by its message!

- Share this message on Twitter, Facebook, or Instagram: **I loved #TheRoarWithin by @BrentAHenderson // @RevellBooks**

- Recommend this book for your church, workplace, book club, or small group.

- Follow Revell on social media and tell us what you like.

RevellBooks

RevellBooks

RevellBooks

pinterest.com/RevellBooks